Teaching Adolescents to Write

The Unsubtle Art of *Naked* Teaching

Lawrence Baines

Mesa State College
Grand Junction, Colorado

Anthony Kunkel

The Cascade School
Whitmore, California

Boston   New York   San Francisco
Mexico City   Montreal   Toronto   London   Madrid   Munich   Paris
Hong Kong   Singapore   Tokyo   Cape Town   Sydney

Series editor: *Aurora Martínez-Ramos*
Editorial assistant: *Annemarie Kennedy*
Senior marketing manager: *Elizabeth Fogarty*
Manufacturing buyer: *JoAnne Sweeney*
Production coordinator: *Pat Torelli Publishing Services*
Cover designer: *Joel Gendron*
Editorial-production service: *Stratford Publishing Services*
Electronic composition: *Stratford Publishing Services*

For related titles and support materials, visit our online catalog at www.ablongman.com.

Library of Congress Cataloging-in-Publication Data
Baines, Lawrence.
 Teaching adolescents to write : the unsubtle art of *naked* teaching /
Lawrence Baines, Anthony Kunkel.
  p. cm.
 Includes bibliographical references.
 ISBN 0-205-35316-9
 1. Language arts (Secondary) I. Kunkel, Anthony J. II. Title.

LB1631 .B155 2003
428'.0071'2--dc21   2002075796

Printed in the United States of America
10 9 8 7 6 5 4 3 2 1   06 05 04 03 02

For Coleen and Robert, who make coming home something special.

—L.B.

For Lynn, who listens to my gypsy whispers.

—A.K.

CONTENTS

5 Novel Expectations: An experience encompassing the entire school year, wherein students elevate personal and peer expectations, develop themselves as critical readers, and author novels for publication—yes, novels   99

6 The Conduct of Life: Teaching philosophy and rhetoric with an edge   117

7 Naked and Fearless   149

8 The Hater Theory: Notes from a sixteen-year-old on the prospect of real life   155

Brian Harris, eleventh grade

Appendix   161

PREFACE

Introduction to an Attitude

You could do worse than to strip in front of your classroom and bare more than just your soul for a change. Teaching naked would definitely be a moment that a good teacher could seize upon, using the unadorned body as a spark for some serious, high-level student engagement. Maybe work in some short readings or creative writing activities on such topics as the rules of societal convention, the paradox of aging, beauty versus superficiality, or perhaps the advantages and drawbacks of freedom of expression.

Teaching is both art and science. Unfortunately, as testing has become the focus for educational reform, the artistic side of teaching has gone by the boards. A teacher is a human being with unique talents and shortcomings who attempts to teach something of value to students—who may well have other things on their minds. To be effective, a teacher must forge some kind of working (hopefully constructive) relationship with each student. However, the complexity of dealing with one highly individualistic American youth is magnified by a factor of thirty, as many secondary classes pack thirty or more students into a classroom. With thirty students per class and six classes per day, a teacher may be responsible for establishing and maintaining relationships with 180 students or more. A further complicating factor in getting to know the students is learning the subtle and variable interrelationships among them. If there is friction or unrest between students (or among groups of students), the teacher's task becomes correspondingly more difficult. Although research can inform and guide practice, to make a difference a teacher must also know how to handle the messy, complicated art of human relationships.

Little wonder, then, that you come home from a day of teaching and collapse on the living room carpet only to waken in an hour or two from a deep, drool-enhanced slumber, exhausted, but with a gnawing sense of panic. Did you bring home that set of papers that need to be graded? What has been eating David, the paunchy sixteen-year-old who sits in the back in third period and has become sullen and grumpy over the past few weeks? Did you forget (once again) to fill out the attendance form and place it properly on the door? You have long since exceeded your allotment for the copier at school, so you need to stop by Kinko's to make copies if you want students to read that article you clipped from *Atlantic Monthly*.

Great amounts of time and money have been spent to help establish minimal competencies and to develop a system of rewards and punishments for schools based upon the results of uniform tests. Unfortunately, no testing, no amount of posturing on issues of curriculum, and no edicts handed down from above concerning conflict resolution, character education, gay rights, or birth control will likely have an impact upon the quality of the relationship between adolescent and teacher. And the quality of that relationship determines so much—achievement, attitude, ambition. Researchers such as Csikszentmihalyi (1993, 1996, with Rathunde & Whalen 1993) and Steinberg (1997) have found that the average adolescent today spends precious little time in one-on-one conversations with his or her parents.

The role of the teacher as adult role model has come to be at least as important as what the teacher actually teaches. To be sure, no student remembers a lesson without recalling the teacher who designed and delivered it. An English teacher serves not only as a model for how to live a life, but also as an exemplar for approaching the acts of reading, writing, speaking, listening, and thinking. Unfortunately, the teacher who descends to the level of worksheet zombie denigrates the power and joy of learning, just as the enthusiastic, caring, well-read bohemian celebrates it.

Currently, momentum is gathering to create schools that are safe havens where standardized exams are the focus for learning. Of course, safety is essential, but many schools have gone overboard in trying to control student behavior by forbidding any but the most mundane and sterile approaches to learning. Incredibly, some school districts mandate that teachers turn in lesson plans coded explicitly to the standardized exam weeks in advance. So much for the "teachable moment."

A coercive, narrow allegiance to testing is no way to inculcate a zeal for learning. One of the goals of any assessment (including those created by Educational Testing Services—ETS), is to ascertain genuine student learning, not the ability to memorize factoids.

In truth, learning is enhanced when it is stimulating and enjoyable. With regard to learning, emotion is not a dirty word. Yet, much of the contemporary curriculum purposefully avoids any emotionally charged issues. Rather than intensifying academic experiences, most schools create rules to inhibit emotion and expression. As D. H. Lawrence noted in *Phoenix II:*

> Emotions by themselves become just a nuisance. The mind by itself becomes just a sterile thing, making everything sterile. So what's to be done? You've got to marry the pair of them. Apart, they are no good. The emotions that have not the approval and inspiration of the mind are just hysterics. The mind without the approval and inspiration of the emotions is just a dry stick, a dead tree, no good for anything unless to make a rod to beat and bully somebody with. (1968, p. 322)

When done right, teaching is intense, exhilarating, and emotionally draining. When done poorly, teaching quickly becomes an exercise in going through the motions, a job rife with illogical mandates, unruly students, and dictatorial administrators. Many teachers spend long hours stewing over aspects of teaching beyond their control (class size, mainstreaming, administrative directives, political flatulence), but such exertions rarely do much good. On the other hand, once a teacher closes the door, he or she has a great deal of control in creating the environment for student learning and student/teacher interactions.

James Moffett described the language arts in terms of symbol systems and how students can manipulate and create those symbol systems—particularly in writing, conversation, and drama. The experiences described in *Teaching Adolescents to Write* use Moffett's conception of a revitalized language arts that helps students "symbolize first- and second-hand experience into an inner world to match against and deal with the outer world" (1968, p. 215) in environments that utilize principles of intense, fulfilling flow experiences (as described by Csikszentmihalyi, 1990, 1996). Many of the activities in *Teaching Adolescents to Write* use proclivities for image-based symbol systems such as video and the Internet to engage students in manipulating language in novel ways.

Through our sometimes unconventional activities, we are trying to create a never-never land where creativity is revered, risk is expected, and awe and wonder become staples of the daily routine. The experiences in *Teaching Adolescents to Write* are founded upon the idea that students need to engage in authentic learning. Over time, you will discover that students remember the lessons when you taught "naked" with more vividness than when you taught "fully clothed." Not only do the experiences in *Teaching Adolescents to Write* satisfy national and state standards, they blow them to smithereens. (Translation: After naked teaching, student scores on the standardized exam should delight even the most curmudgeonly administrator.)

How *Teaching Adolescents to Write* Is Organized

Because it is difficult to gather momentum in single, one-shot, fifty-minute classes, we have created this book around experiences that are easily adapted to ninety- or one hundred–minute blocks. These experiences require the teacher to be bold in charting and navigating the classroom environment, to teach in innovative ways, and to always give the student the opportunity to explore beyond the boundaries of the structured assignment. We provide student samples every step of the way, which we designate by a screened box:

Student Sample

We included student samples to show real outcomes, and we wanted you to have examples to share with your own students. The student work we selected is from the hearts and minds of a variety of students—rich, poor, AP, remedial, regular, white, African American, Hispanic, Asian. Some of the reviewers for this book told us that we probably used too many examples of student work. So, it won't hurt our feelings if you skip a few of these, but please don't ignore all the student work. Much of it is simply incredible.

We also include a shipload of handouts. These instructions and activities were used in our classrooms, and we reproduce them verbatim in the text. Handouts are designated by nonshaded boxes:

HANDOUT

The experiences described in *Teaching Adolescents to Write* include our own sometimes rambling narratives, unedited student work, and handouts. The idea behind offering such excruciating detail is that it allows you to see the results of our thinking so that you can modify our ideas according to your own talents and dispositions. Regardless, the experiences involve much planning and depend upon the careful choreography of a variety of prompts, readings, and assignments over time. The experiences usually begin by engaging students with a fun, easy activity and then build toward more complex tasks as student interest and involvement grow.

In Chapter 1, The Essential Environment, we describe how to build the necessary foundation for an exciting, creative classroom. As the student letter in the chapter attests, "It's an extremely hard class . . . but looking back, you'll realize that all that crazy work just to pull off an 80 was worth it."

In Chapter 2, Growing Up, Baines describes how an encounter with an incorrigible student who had a penchant for murdering him (in compositions) led him to reformulate his approach to teaching writing. Baines works off of tenets from Kinneavy's *A Theory of Discourse* (1971) to create a writing-intensive experience that engages students by appealing to one of their main interests—themselves. Chapter 2 includes a matrix of sixteen different writing assignments, suggestions for predetermining audience and purpose, and some amazing compositions from the hearts and hands of twelve-year-olds.

In Chapter 3, AP Aliens, students work collaboratively to create descriptions of the demographics and sociology of alien races, and in the process are introduced to the notion of the archetypal hero (Campbell 1972, 1973; Osbon 1991) and a variety of origin myths. We use the appeal of alien cultures to get students to create sophisticated compositions using specific rhetorical techniques. Each new step builds upon a previous one, and the experience culminates with a critical analysis and a persuasive-writing paper that will either save students' invented alien races or annihilate them.

Chapter 4, Screenplays, uses the lures of Hollywood, money, and image-based media to engage students in drama, collaborative writing, and a careful examination of texts. Over the course of three to five weeks, students write several papers, read numerous literary works and screenplays, examine the process of adapting a book to film, and write, shoot, produce, and present two videos.

Chapter 5, Novel Expectations, probably has one of the longest subtitles in the history of publishing: An Experience Encompassing the Entire School Year,

Wherein Students Elevate Personal and Peer Expectations, Develop Themselves as Critical Readers, and Author Novels for Publication—Yes, Novels. In this chapter, we explain how to get students to *enthusiastically* write a 200- to 300-page novel over the course of a year. It is testimony to the success of the experience in improving students' writing that twenty-two of Kunkel's students in the class were published in national professional or literary journals that year. Of the several students who sent their books to prospective publishers, a few received encouraging letters, including requests for revision and resubmission.

In Chapter 6, Conduct of Life, students read selected philosophical writings, poetry, a short story, and nonfiction articles from contemporary journals; write and recite poems and essays; draw, color, and take photographs; shoot and edit videotape; and create a soundtrack. As a final step, students reconceptualize their original papers to include the images, sounds, and themes of the video in a revised work. The revision must be communicated through words only.

In Chapter 7, we take you to the front lines to show you how a naked and fearless teacher might respond to the usual chaos of an overexuberant class (nice teacher lingo for "the class from hell"). Hey—we didn't even have to think up this scenario; it was third period a few years ago. Some teachers with more sanity and less chutzpah would resign at the end of the day after such a class, but you, being Naked and Fearless, seize the moment and create a memorable lesson. At least, that's what we are hoping. We end Chapter 7 with all kinds of back slapping and teacher bonding–type talk in the hope that your resolution to teach naked and fearless will endure, even after the principal calls you on the carpet and starts yelling at you for teaching something of value to your students.

For those of you who are planning to skip over the student samples in the shaded boxes, we have included an essay by a sixteen-year-old angst-ridden junior entitled, "The Hater Theory: Notes from a Sixteen-year-old on the Prospect of Real Life," disguised as Chapter 8. In "Hater Theory," the student (Brian Harris) describes the sense of angst, detachment, and boredom that seems pervasive in schools today. While the essay is sarcastic and brooding, it also has the unmistakable ring of authenticity. The challenge for secondary teachers of English is to engage students like Harris with assignments that are worthy of his time—experiences that stimulate the intellect but also acknowledge the soul.

Tragically, much of teaching in high school these days is directed toward transforming students into complacent, numb "walking data machines." Norman Cousins writes, "Education tends to be diagrammatic and categorical, opening up no sluices in the human imagination on the wonder of beauty of their unique estate in the cosmos. Little wonder that it becomes so easy for our young to regard human hurt casually or to be uninspired by the magic of sensitivity" (1996, p. 69). Little wonder that students like Harris note the disparity between the lockstep factoid factory of school and the tumult of life outside its walls with such dark cynicism.

Naked teaching is about transcending conformity, using emotion in the cause of intellect, and redesigning the classroom environment so that it percolates with creativity and excitement. Naked teaching is about recognizing your strengths and your passions, and then passing them on. Naked teaching is about shirking the inconsequential blather that poses as educational reform and instead building productive, humanistic one-on-one relationships with students. Naked teaching is about cultivating an appetite for knowledge, honing an appreciation for art, and teaching like you really mean it.

At this point, it probably would be wise if we reiterated that naked teaching is more a state of mind than a curriculum guide. Literal nudity is completely optional.

Acknowledgments

Our appreciation goes to the following reviewers for their helpful comments on the manuscript: Pamela Sissi Carroll, Florida State University; Diane Green, Mississippi State University; Marian Matthews, Eastern New Mexico University; and Sara Tyler, Tarleton State University.

REFERENCES

Campbell, J. (1972). *Myths to Live By.* New York: Penguin.
——— (1973). *The Hero with a Thousand Faces.* Princeton, New Jersey: Princeton/Bollingen.
Cousins, N. (1996). In P. Lorie and M. Mascetti, eds., *The Quotable Spirit.* New York: Macmillan, 69.
Csikszentmihalyi, M. (1990). *Flow.* New York: HarperCollins.
——— (1993). *The Evolving Self: A Psychology for the Third Millennium.* New York: HarperCollins.
——— (1996). *Creativity: Flow and the Psychology of Discovery and Invention.* New York: Harper-Collins.
———, Rathunde, K., and Whalen, S. (1993). *Talented Teens.* New York: Cambridge University Press.
Kinneavy, J. (1971). *A Theory of Discourse.* New York: W.W. Norton.
Lawrence, D. H. (1968). *Phoenix II: Uncollected, Unpublished, and Other Prose Works.* New York: Viking.
McCourt, F. (1999). *'Tis.* New York: Simon & Schuster.
Moffett, J. (1968). *Teaching the Universe of Discourse.* Boston: Houghton Mifflin.
Osbon, D., ed. (1991). *A Joseph Campbell Companion.* New York: HarperCollins.
Steinberg, L. (1997). *Beyond the Classroom.* New York: Simon & Schuster.

There was a confusion and a darkness in my head and I had to understand what I was doing in this classroom or get out. If I had to stand before those five classes I couldn't let days dribble by in the routine of high school grammar, spelling, vocabulary, digging for the deeper meaning in poetry, bits of literature doled out for the multiple choice tests that would follow so that universities can be supplied with the best and the brightest. I had to begin enjoying the act of teaching and the only way I could do that was to start over, teach what I loved and to hell with the curriculum.

—McCourt, 1999, *'Tis,* p. 340

1

The Essential Environment

Establishing tone, minimizing disruptions, and fostering creativity in the classroom

Reality Principle: *n. Awareness of and adjustment to environmental demands in a manner that assures ultimate satisfaction of instinctual needs.*
—The American Heritage High School Dictionary, Third Edition

Much of the time, teaching has little to do with theory. My experience has been that theory may look good on paper, but it fails to account for reality. That's why they call it *theory*. Of course, it's useful to know what "the experts" are saying, but you can't rely wholly on people who have never met you or your students. I'll concede that, as professionals, educators have a certain responsibility to be familiar with the research being done within the field (past and present), but knowledge of theories does not a teacher make. Knowing that a student is a visual learner and how to engage a visual learner will do teachers little good if they are not prepared to consider that this "visual learner" is also (for example) being physically and mentally abused on a daily basis by an alcoholic father, and that the student couldn't give a crap about Kurt Vonnegut's writing or the grade that's attached to reading it. So it goes. Theory may serve as a good starting place, but sooner or later you will have to shed some sweat and tears. To get inside the hearts and minds of students, you must learn to rely upon your intuition as much as your intellect.

I'm not going to pretend to have an answer here. The problems of apathy and opposition are the challenges of today's classroom. I'm not suggesting that teachers turn their backs on the research that has been done in education, but let's be realistic, oftentimes such research seems to have been conducted on the planet Utopia where all students are happy, eager, well-adjusted angels. What I know is that each student in my class is unique and that each classroom has a personality of its own. As a teacher, you never want to ignore students' needs so that your pet theory remains intact.

Today's adolescents are extremely perceptive individuals. They have good instincts and are well aware of which teachers are in tune with their realities, and which teachers are not. I try to be on level footing with my students, and I find that most of them *are* in fact easily engaged and ready to learn. In past years I have come to realize that the world I create within my classroom is not what one might expect to find in a typical high-school-English setting. Yet what I do, and the kind of classroom I try to create, will seem nothing more than common sense to many. That is exactly what it is.

For all intents and purposes, I am a writing teacher. It makes sense for me to think of my classroom as a writing environment. When I write with a specific goal in mind, it helps me to focus on who my audience is. When I set up my classroom before the year begins, I have specific goals in mind, and once again, I focus on my audience. Just as I am writing this chapter specifically with fellow teachers and prospective teachers in mind, I set up my classes specifically with my students in mind. It is my ritual to emblazon my walls with posters that will unlock the imagination—words of wit, lively colors, paintings by Michael Parkes, photographs of Albert Einstein, Frumious Bandersnatches, pictures of paradoxes. I want my students inspired and thinking; I don't tolerate apathy.

The beginning is critical. Just as the writer must grab the reader's attention at the onset, the writing teacher must grab the student's attention from day one. As a writing teacher, I expose myself completely with the first sentence I utter. From the beginning, I hope to establish tone. The tone in the first paragraph of this chapter was intended to be serious; so is the tone of my teaching during the first few weeks of class. I am a staunch advocate of the "intimidation" approach within the early weeks of school.

Let me pause here for a moment and explain what I mean by "intimidate." For the first two weeks of class, I am the teacher who overreacts. If students look at me wrong, I give them detention. If they argue, I write them up. If they talk while I'm talking, I send them out. But I do so only long enough to implement some interesting and engaging activities. It is amazing how well the class as a whole responds when suddenly they are having fun. From my experience, if classroom control is not established at the onset, chances are that it will not be gained for the remainder of the year. Most students do not forget the first few weeks in my class, and it is easy for me to shift gears back into authoritarian mode if the need arises. My goal is to establish an environment where expectations are high, disruptions are not tolerated, and a strong work ethic is the norm.

The reality is that most of my new students do not know me when they walk into the classroom, unless by reputation. They are as curious to find out what their perimeters are and what I will tolerate as I am to find out what I can expect from each of them. Therefore, I make it easy—I declare to them on the first day of school that I will tolerate nothing less than brilliance, hard work, respect, and their continual growth as individuals and as writers. Tone. It is one thing for a teacher to stand in front of the class and pontificate about how strict they are going to be, but it helps to have some eye-opening examples that illustrate the point.

Figure 1.1 is a copy of a letter that I have my students write at the end of each year. The idea is for them to write a letter to the upcoming students, telling them a

FIGURE 1.1   Eye-opener Letter

Dear Student,

I'm not going drag things out, I'm just going to be upfront with you... RUN!, Run like you've never run before and don't stop running, move down, change teachers, change schools; do anything you can to get away from this class and Mr. Kunkle!! Unless... unless you are willing to buckle down and work insainly hard this year, unless you want to improve your ~~writing~~ writing by remarkable amounts and want to feel like I do right now, proud. I have been in Mr. Kunkle's 11th grade AP English class at Rome High all year, and spent most of it slaving over a computer, only to have it mess up and loose all of the 3,000 words I had written. I have pulled three all-nighters for this class, have read seven books, worked really hard on an extra credit assignment only to get one point, made a complete alien species only to get demolished by another, and wrote a novel. It's an extreamly hard class, but when you are where I am now and ~~am~~ are looking back, you'll realized that all that crazy work just to pull off an 80 was worth it. Just do the work and DON'T PROCRASTINATE! Read the novels during the ~~wea~~ week, not the day after prom, it doesn't work! Save your novels many, many times, on to the hard drive and the disk. oh yeah, DO NOT try to be the big guy and attack another group's aliens, that doesn't work either. All I can tell you is to work insainly hard in this class. It's a good class, it just takes a lot of work! Good Luck!

Best Regards,
Jessie Williamson

little bit about my class, what they can expect, and me. These I use as my eye-openers.

Normally, my students have a good time writing these letters, having survived my class, and remembering when they were reading the letters from the previous year's students. I begin my first day by passing out these letters, giving the students a chance to read them silently, and then asking for volunteers to read theirs aloud. The nice thing about this activity is that I have been able to select specific letters that I hope will get across the message I intend. Usually there are several volunteers to read. This is a different kind of reading for the students; there is no intimidating literature or textbook in front of them, only a letter from a fellow student, often someone they know or have seen around. While they are hearing about my expectations and the serious amount of writing that is ahead of them as their classmates read words that were written by their peers, I am watching them exchange glances and shake and nod their heads. I am also finding out who some of the better readers are.

When a good representation of what they will be going through has been read, I confirm everything they have just heard. If I'm lucky, some of them will have also noticed the tone of respect and admiration that many of my previous students had developed over time, as well as some playfulness and words of hope—I wish for there to always be hope. At this point, my expectations and their perimeters have been stated and restated, and all I have left to do is follow up with any who wish to test the validity of what they have heard. If I am lucky, one or two will do so quickly, and I will write them up equally as quickly. I do not take pleasure in writing up students, but at the onset of the year, if I wish to have a working environment, I need complete control, and making examples is a great deterrent to any of those students who are contemplating whether they wish to participate or not.

Having established myself as the authority figure that so many of them often take pride in rebelling against, I will use the next few weeks to engage them in a variety of writing activities. The first few days are always designed to be enjoyable and to assure instant feedback and some successful writing. What I have found to be an effective beginning is to start with some short creative writing activities that leave time for oral readings.

One of my favorite first activities is a lesson called "creating man," a lesson that asks students to imagine and write about a fictional character. It is easy to walk the students through, one sentence at a time, and when it is complete, most students will have written something unlike anything they have written in the past. This is where the first major shift from a typical English classroom to a writing environment takes place. With the completion of the activity, I collect all the writing samples and read them aloud. Adolescents are very self-conscious, and I find that reading their work out loud myself (to begin with) will make them more comfortable when it is time for them to read their work at a later date. Most students are anxious to hear their invented characters read, and many of them are stunned at the depth and imagination of their peers. Following are two samples of what can be expected from an average ninth grader with such an activity.

#1   Jake Blanchard placed the gun gently against his forehead. Why did it have to be like this, he thought? He stepped closer to the window and gazed longingly at the city of lights below him. He remembered the birth of his first son, and smiled softly. Jake took the gun from his forehead, shook his head for a moment, then placed the gun in against the roof of his mouth and pulled the trigger.

#2   Keven Bluntweed grabbed the papers from the counter. With any luck at all I'll be higher than heaven before the night is out, he thought. He made his way out of his apartment and quietly approached the door of the man with the stash. He thought of his ex and wondered who she'd be sleeping with tonight. He opened the door to the stranger's house, saw the blood on the wall, and never heard the bullet that killed him.

Both of these samples were written within the thirty minutes allotted for this portion of the assignment, yet both demonstrate a mature and graphic look at the world these kids live in and the way their imaginations work. When read aloud, student writing elicits an appreciation from classmates that is not soon forgotten by the authors. Also, many students will have just written something unlike anything they had ever written before. After such an activity, the students are excited about what they have just done and enthusiastic to see what will come next.

I should note that on occasion I have been criticized for allowing my students to write violent or graphic scenes, but I fail to see how writing can be considered an art if students are not allowed to use it as a means to express and interpret the world around them as they see it. I draw lines when it comes to unnecessary language and graphic sex, but a realistic view of the world they live in is not something that I consider appropriate for censorship. Most of my students find this freedom extremely liberating, and I find it essential to creating a true writing environment.

Up to this point, the activities have been primarily one-period writing activities, most of them followed with oral presentations, some mandatory, most voluntary. When I feel that my students have begun to appreciate their own writing and the writing of their classmates, I seek to evolve their environment into one more disposed toward collaboration. Once I change my classroom into a cooperative setting, the students will often spend the rest of the year within a specific writing group, barring any major personality conflicts or lack of participation. I believe in cooperative learning, but I also am aware of the pitfalls that can come with it. Students are very used to being "grouped," and all too often the more conscientious students cringe at the thought because they are used to doing all the work for several other students in their group. To ensure participation from all members, I go to great lengths to establish the groups, and then do the footwork to ensure each student is aware of my expectations regarding their individual participation within the group. I spend a good deal of time deciding which students to pair up, considering not only their individual skill levels, but their personalities as well. With a large class it will more than likely be necessary to create groups of four students. When possible, I try to place the students into smaller groups, three being ideal.

Based on my observations and experiences putting groups together, I have discovered several combinations that work effectively. First and foremost, each group will need a leader—a student who is fairly reliable, typically a better writer than the other group members, and a student who doesn't mind the added responsibility of helping their groupmates. With each class, the first thing I do is decide how many groups I will have, and then I determine specific students who will act as group leaders for each of those groups. From this point I am ready to begin grouping. Combinations that work are often difficult to establish, and too often I have one group with which I don't feel entirely comfortable. However, I reserve the right to change my mind and adjust each group as I see fit through the course of the year.

Pairing close friends sometimes works if the students in question have shown an interest in the work being done and a genuine enthusiasm for what each is writing. The upside to such a group is that they will be comfortable with each other and often work well and creatively together. The downside occurs if they have a falling out beyond the walls of the classroom, as does happen. Also, these groups tend to be easily distracted with matters unrelated to the class—something I do not tolerate.

For the class that is strongly male dominated (and there always seems to be one), I have discovered what I like to call the "alpha group." This concept is one of the most unlikely of success stories, but time and again, I have been surprised by the quality of work that comes from such a grouping. This is a group of all male students, usually athletes, who ideally should not be scheduled in the same class together, let alone in the same group. The critical element to success in this group is the group leader, or the "alpha male." This group is run in much the same way as an offense on a football team. The alpha male is essentially the quarterback, and the teacher the coach. When three mischievous, oversized adolescent males see a friend whom they respect knuckle down and take care of business, it is amazing how easily they follow suit. When this group begins competing with the other groups, the competitive instinct is enjoyable to watch. One point that should be mentioned: If this type of group does not respond positively, it will more than likely be an instant disaster, and an immediate adjustment will be needed. This is not always a bad thing, though, because it allows those group members who are pleased with their groups the opportunity to witness what happens when cooperation crumbles.

Another grouping that I have found to be effective is what I call the "beauty and the beast" group. Most of my classes have had the classic rebel-without-a-clue student. These types are the underachievers, the extremely intelligent students who seem to be lacking in discipline and motivation. Too often these students have horror stories instead of families. These students can be serious discipline problems if they are bored or upset. The concept behind this group is the matching of opposites. Sometimes this can be intimidating, but more often than not, I have witnessed unique and enduring friendships develop. For example, this group will have a leader (a "beauty") who is typically quiet and shy, grade-conscious, calm, and often easily embarrassed. The underachiever (the "beast") in this type of group should be the gender opposite of the leader. I am not a psychologist, nor do I pretend to be, but I have witnessed many angst-filled and angry adolescents turn into brilliant writers in this type of group. I have also witnessed many occasions when the entire class has come to respect a person for the power and the honesty of their writing, where before the person had been completely ostracized. The "beasts" that are present in your classroom may well have the potential to become passionate writers with the right partners.

Other groups that work well really become a matter of common sense, and after spending a few weeks having the class write (and read what they write) as individuals, you should be able to determine which combinations will work and which will not. The specific groupings that I have discussed are more a means to deter any potential problems and maximize the class as a place for creativity and writing. Of course, a teacher's personality will also determine what types of groups work and what types do not. The idea is to provide an environment for collaboration, peer involvement, and tutoring for those students who are sometimes reluctant to ask a teacher for help.

Once groups have been set, I start the day by arranging the desks into clusters (fully planning on leaving them that way for the remainder of the year) and writing the group assignments on the board. I also include a note that the groups are not negotiable, and that if students fail to pull their load within any group, they will be removed from the group setting and, in all likelihood, will fail the class. When the groups have found their seats and settled in, I give students Handout 1.1.

This activity is not my invention (I ripped it off from Baines, who ripped it off from a book called *Values Clarification,* by Sidney B. Simon), but the circumstances and most of the characters are original ideas that have grown and evolved over the course of years. Once the groups have looked over the handout, I give them about half the class time to compile a written list of their chosen survivors. I also require them to include a written explanation for why they chose each of the individuals that they did. The last thing I require is a written summary from each group describing the world fifty years later based on what their characters may have created once they were freed from the shelter.

The idea is not so much to assign a written exercise as it is to give the groups a goal and a deadline. My objective is to introduce each group into a situation that requires them to begin interacting as a group, to do some intelligent arguing and debating, and to learn what it feels like to work cooperatively. When the class is half over, I ask the students to make oral presentations. Each group is to stand up and take turns telling of their selections, the reasons for their selections, and the summaries of their anticipated future. Usually during this phase of the activity the class becomes very animated, pointing out flaws in logic and disagreeing with specific selections.

HANDOUT **1.1**

Cooperative Activity—Chinese Civil War

Suddenly, China broke out in civil war. Political extremists came to control a nuclear stockpile and began launching missiles at the U.S. One year later the world is in ruins. After the initial missiles landed in the U.S., we retaliated strongly, obliterating China completely. Russia then began launching missiles at the U.S., causing more casualties. Europe began launching at Russia; then they came under fire from Iraq. Israel attacked Iraq, but the fallout from such a close target destroyed them as well. Now radar is down, satellites have become useless, survivors have turned into cannibals, and civilization as it once was known has ended. What is left of the United States government is a group of students who must make a decision. The students have relocated to the small college town of Arcata, California, where the previous leaders had put together a project to save mankind from extinction. An underwater tube was built from Humboldt Bay to a shelter that sits 1,000 feet below the surface of the ocean, miles from shore, and undetectable to any subs that may have survived. This shelter will house six people for seven years, then will rise to the surface and drift to the shore. There is only enough food, water, and oxygen to last six people seven years, so it is not possible to send more than six into the shelter.

It is up to the students to decide who goes into the shelter. On the flight over to Arcata, the students' plane unknowingly went through a radioactive storm and now all members of the student group have radiation poison, and it will not be possible for any of them to go into the shelter. The group of scientists who were originally scheduled to go into the shelter was on the wrong side of a misfired missile and they are all missing in action. Unfortunately, there is only the list of these fifteen survivors to choose from, and the gates to the shelter entrance will be sealed in one hour, so the group must choose the six candidates to enter the shelter and save mankind from extinction, quickly.

At this point in the war, it becomes essential that the group members cooperate with each other, as well as respect each other's opinions. In making a decision, all group members must agree, and if *any* group member wishes to veto a candidate, the entire group must go along—there is no majority rule. You are that group. The only candidates you have to choose from are on the list below. All you have to go on is what's on the list— no additional information is available. Remember, those you choose will return in seven years to repopulate the world.

Shelter Candidates

Dr. Amoc—A 32-year-old male doctor who has been catatonic since the death of his wife and kids the month before. He is currently a vegetable who cannot even feed himself.

Ricky Slive—A 27-year-old carpenter who believes Satan is the only true god.

Dusky Ruth—A 33-year-old female botanist who is unable to have children.

Sister Mary Catherine—A 44-year-old Catholic nun.

Disco Beano—A 56-year-old man who randomly begins singing disco oldies at the top of his lungs and then dances while he sings—all day and night long.

Phil Data—A 37-year-old architect who thinks Hitler had the right idea.

Zeke Allen—A 64-year-old Jewish rabbi.

Adelle Purity—A 1-month-old baby girl whose mother passed on the previous night.

Wanda Good—A 29-year-old female psychiatrist who was born blind, as was her mother and her mother's mother.

Armondo Pepper—A 43-year-old master chef who is gay.

Jake Spade—A 26-year-old professional hunter who has been convicted for kidnapping, rape, and assault.

Cindy Smith—A 16-year-old diabetic.

Rock Stone—A 15-year-old male drug addict who is HIV-positive.

Neila Borg—A 21-year-old librarian who believes that she was stolen as a child and taken from her home planet, Borgonia.

Nick Chance—A 7-year-old boy with Down's syndrome.

During the students' first week working together as a group, each new day brings a new cooperative activity. One day I may have them write tag stories—stories that are written one sentence at a time before they are rotated to the next group member. The next day they may play a game involving vocabulary. Each day, though, they are challenged as a group, and each group is given the task of competing against the other groups in the class. It is during this first week that I spend a good deal of time insisting that the group leaders work with their group members, proofreading their work, helping them interpret problems, and pointing out mistakes that they will need to correct. By doing this, I hope to reinforce to my classes that I expect quality at all times, that I will hold the group leaders responsible for their group's successes and failures, and that each student has a writing support group from which they can seek help, without having to wait for a conference with me.

Once the groups are established and students seem comfortable with them, I abruptly cease the cooperative activities and begin what will be the first of many major individual writing projects. Up until this point, much of what I have been doing is laying a foundation for what is to come. Much of that foundation will rely on the students—first, that they are willing to write, and second, that they are in an environment where writing is taken seriously, where students are genuinely interested in each other's writing. This is the essential environment.

The first major piece of individual writing done in my classes is always a reflective essay. I choose the reflective essay because it often elicits strong reactions from students. My teaching objective with the reflective essay is that the students will write an extended piece of nonfiction based on a specific event in their lives—something that holds some emotional meaning. One of my primary criteria is that the tone of the essay clearly convey the emotion that is attached to the memory.

I got the idea for the lesson from an exercise in John Gardner's book *The Art of Fiction*. Basically, the students are to describe an imaginary house from three emotional perspectives (three separate pieces of writing), and within each description are to convey the emotion without telling what it is. I use this lesson at the onset of my reflective essay project. Many students will write something surprisingly good, and most will wish to read their papers aloud. On occasion, I choose to read students' papers myself and have the students guess which emotion is being conveyed.

When I am ready to begin the project, I allow a day for the students to brainstorm. I have not told them what they will be doing at this point, so the brainstorming in itself becomes an activity in reflection. If there is an appropriate outdoor setting, I take my classes outside. The students are instructed to find a spot where they can be by themselves (yet within my sight), and then to assemble a list of every event in their lives that has had some type of impact on them. With each event they list, they are to write the emotion that is associated with it. Many of them will have events that they do not wish to discuss or that they do not wish anyone to know about. I address this by acknowledging that I'm aware of some "instances" in many of their lives that are private, and that if they wish to list those, the choice is up to them. I inform them that I will not require such memories to be shared, but as a teacher, I will need at some point to read what they are writing. During this activity, many students will become reflective, and many will create a long, intricate list, one memory leading into the next.

Once the students have their lists of memories, I inform them of the assignment (usually the next day). I tell them that they are to select one memory, or event, from their lists, and that they are to write a creative essay that tells about it. I instruct them of my primary criterion—creating tone to convey the emotion. My methods may seem unconventional, but the results speak for themselves. I see no point in teaching a student to write from the heart if I am not interested in what their hearts have to say.

While I do not encourage students to write of personal matters that may require me to involve the school counselors, I do ask them to reach deep within themselves and find something powerful to write about. The death of a relative or friend is a topic I mention that may elicit some strong emotions, as would a traumatic event from childhood. If students begin to cry while writing, I know that they are writing from their hearts, and that writing will never be the same for them again. Writing will suddenly have gotten personal. On occasion, I have had to present an essay to the guidance counselor to get legal advice, and I have had essays that crossed the line to "inappropriate" sexual content. However, they were attempts at art and connecting words with experiences, and they were authentic expressions. When an essay becomes inappropriate, it is not difficult to have a student do a rewrite, toning things down a bit, and usually the finished product is a pretty decent piece of writing. When I assign the reflective essay, most of the papers I receive are good—better than anything most of the students have ever written.

I try not to put a page length on the assignment, but I ask students to try and keep the rough drafts under twenty pages. Most of them laugh at this, but many of them find that requirement restricting. Those students who are used to doing only the minimum, if anything at all, become confused with an assignment where there is only a maximum requirement. They may even become intimidated by witnessing so many of their peers writing lengthy rough drafts. For the occasional student who calls me over to show me a finished two-page rough draft, I'll read it, say that it looks like a good outline, and suggest that they get started writing the actual essay. All students are informed that grammar, spelling, and mechanics on the rough drafts are secondary to what is actually being written. All writing done on the rough draft portion of this project is done in class, over the course of several days—no essays leave the classroom, no essays get lost, and no student has an excuse not to be working. During the writing of the rough drafts, my classroom becomes a functioning writer's workshop.

Getting all students to finish at the same time is impossible. Letting them know that it's time to finish the rough draft and giving them one extra day is a way of forcing a deadline. For those students writing very lengthy pieces, I do make exceptions, and I allow students I know to be reliable to take their essays home on the last few days of the writing workshop.

Once the rough drafts are done, it is time for peer critiques. Peer critiquing is where the group setting becomes extremely useful, and it is where many students will become much more developed writers over the course of the year. Many of the weaker writers will be intimidated by the peer critiques, and they will need to be encouraged to voice their opinions in writing. When we first begin peer critiques, many students will write things like "good plot," or "great description." I begin my peer critiquing session by writing such phrases on the chalkboard and underlining them. When I have all the students' attention, I tell them that if they are brave enough to write anything so simplistic on a critique, I will expect a full explanation as to exactly what it is that makes it a "great description," including examples. During the first critiquing session, I keep myself busy telling students to explain their comments in more detail. If I set up the first session correctly, the subsequent critiquing sessions will be much more constructive. Because the critiquing is such a new concept to many of them, I provide a handout that allows for specific comments. Handout 1.2 is what I use for the reflective essays.

For a typical peer critiquing session, I have each group pass their essays to the left or right and ask that each student read the essay carefully. Once they have read the essay, I give them the critiquing handout. Under most circumstances peer critiquing takes the entire period. When all students are done, they hand back the essays along with the comments on the handout. I encourage them to talk about the essays and ask questions.

Occasionally students write something extremely personal on their reflective essays; for these students, I verify that it is as personal as they have indicated and excuse them from having their essays read. I have had instances where these students have indicated that they have a friend who is already aware of the event they have written about, and if I feel comfortable, I will place these students together for this peer critiquing session. There have also been instances where some students did not want anyone reading their essay, simply because they were embarrassed.

H A N D O U T **1.2**
Reflective Essay Peer Critique Sheet

Name of person being critiqued_____

Your Name_____

Please read your fellow group member's reflective essay and, using this handout, make intelligent comments that will help them to make this a better essay during revision. Do not write simple phrases, but instead write comments that explain the problems you found, as well as suggestions that would help.

Describe what you liked most about what was written within the essay:

_____

_____

_____

_____

_____

_____

Give at least two detailed, constructive suggestions that could improve the essay:

_____

_____

_____

_____

_____

_____

Describe the tone you felt this essay was trying to convey, and use an example from the essay to illustrate where you felt this tone was the strongest:

_____

_____

_____

_____

_____

_____

If you had to grade this essay right now (between 1 and 100), what grade would you give it, and what comments would you attach explaining your grade?

_____

_____

_____

_____

_____

_____

I make it very clear that in my writing workshops all students will be required to share their work and their analysis of their classmates' work. I do not excuse them from the session unless they become visibly distressed, at which point I excuse them with the understanding that they will be expected to participate in the next one.

The final phase of the reflective essays is the revision process. As with other assignments for this project, I expect a great deal of revision to take place. Once again, students may use only class time to revise. Normally, I give the students two full class periods to revise, asking them to mark up their drafts and to make changes directly on them. During the revision phase, I begin to rely strongly on group leaders. I ask the leaders to take an active role in helping their group members with wording, sentences, and mechanics when needed. Normally, when it is obvious that group members are doing what I asked, I allow them the luxury of taking their work home if needed, and I give them an extra day or two for the finished product. If I have succeeded in my early endeavors to create an atmosphere conducive to creativity and writing, what I will witness at this point is a truly cooperative setting, a classroom where students are engaged with their own writing, as well as the writings of their peers. Disruptions at this point are a rarity, as unwelcome by the students as they are by me.

With the conclusion of the revision comes the final manuscript. How I require these depends strongly on the class. For example, an eleventh-grade AP Language and Composition class will need to submit a final copy that is typed, formatted, has an appropriate cover sheet, and includes the rough draft paperclipped to the back. A regular-level ninth-grade class, on the other hand, will be given time to write a neat copy in the classroom, but I still hesitate to let them take manuscripts home for worry of never seeing them again.

Once all essays are completed, students give oral presentations. These can take an extremely long time, but if every student wishes to read, I let them. Because most of my students have never written anything so extensive and personal, they experience a sense of accomplishment and pride about their writing that is unfamiliar. I do on occasion make oral readings mandatory, but once again, if a student has written something that is extremely personal, I deal with them on an individual basis, more often than not excusing them from reading aloud. It is not uncommon for a student reading a story about the death of someone close to deteriorate to tears by the time they have finished. In these cases, many of their classmates are in tears as well. I do not make them read when the topic is death, and I offer to let them sit, but most will struggle through, pouring out their hearts, insisting on finishing what they started. Below are excerpts from a reflective essay by a student who recently lost her mother to cancer.

Mother
by Anita

Sitting on the high school baseball field, the painful memory of my mother's cancerous death painted my views once again.

I quietly stepped into the long, twisting hallway from the elevator. My sister softly pushed me forward in the direction of my mother's room. My feet made tiny movements on the cold floor, until at last I stopped in front of a bare, wooden door that towered many feet above the tiny child I was. I pushed the cracked door open, allowing the light from the corridor to escape the hallway and illuminate the dim hospital cell. In this cell my mother slept in confinement with occasional jerking movements and convulsions of pain.

The light first passed over my brother who sat staring at the floor with his face buried in his large hands. As I continued to open the door, the light revealed my stepfather holding and caressing the life that lingered in my mother's hands. I saw him shadow over her bed and kiss her forehead, then quickly he straightened when he finally heard our muffled voices. My brother did not look up right away, however. Instead, his hands crept farther up his hair; his elbows still steadily placed on his legs.

As if we all understood his sadness, no one spoke of his isolation. Instead we left him to his lonely position. He appeared so grown to me, although he was only fourteen, and I just eight. . . .

. . . My face quickly tensed and I squeezed my eyes to release the tears. My mouth ached from holding it open to cry. No sound came out this time, but I heard my screams being pushed back into the depths of my heart. I did not want her to slip away and leave me. Memories of us singing together flashed into the dusty light, the melody drifting just below my consciousness. "You are my sunshine, my only sunshine . . . " I willed for the darkness to retreat. I wanted to be her sunshine again. . . .

. . . I regret never turning around that night. I wish I touched my mother or at least looked at her one last time. Instead, I continued to carry myself from the room as if my time with my mother would not be stolen. Endless nights of praying filled my life's meaningless schedule for many months after my mother's death. Her life's ending left me sore with regret and emptiness. My last memory of my mother stained my pillow for years.

One night, long after my mother's death, my grandfather shared these profound words with me, "You can only experience as much happiness to the same extent that you have experienced true pain." I know that I still have great heights left to reach. I am climbing up from the deepest valleys.

Once I have reached this point in my classes, I have established the writer's environment that I feel is so critical to success. In such an environment, the attitudes are constructive, and the students are receptive to writing and learning. I will spend the entire year combining cooperative activities with lengthy individual writing projects. Few of the major writing projects will be as emotional as the reflective essays, but somewhere along the way, the students will begin to take their writing more seriously (which includes a personal interest in improving their mechanics), and each project will, in its own way, add a little more depth to what they are able to do as writers. So it goes.

Assessment

For the first few weeks, my purpose is to create a perception about writing that is unique. I want writing to become an activity that is its own reward. At the onset, very little emphasis is placed on spelling and grammar. When the students are writing, I sit with them, reading what they have written and giving them immediate feedback, always giving praise for a good phrase or unique adjective. On finished essays and stories, I comment extensively on the positives, make note of weaknesses that I've identified, and score them on individual expectations, abilities, and effort.

In the first few weeks of class, I work on description, tone, and word choice. My rubric for the reflective essay places an emphasis on the use of descriptive adjectives, tone, depth, and quality of the writing, as well as the revision effort shown on the rough draft. The typical C paper reflects an honest attempt at descriptive writing, whereas the A paper demonstrates a deeper understanding of tone and mood through description as well as mechanics and varied sentence structure.

As the class progresses through the year, my expectations for the students as individual writers progresses as well. Without fail, the students begin to take notice of their weaknesses, and self-address whatever grammatical and mechanical errors they repeatedly have struggled with. When students want to write quality compositions, they learn mechanics and grammar without whining. When a student begins to show the first vestiges of style, I direct them to literature that I think will resonate with them. When a student chooses to write a composition in which he or she uses nonstandard English for effect, I never dissuade them. The fact that they are beginning to explore different ways to be effective speaks volumes in and of itself.

REFERENCES

Baines, L., and Kunkel, A. (2000). *Going Bohemian: Activities to Engage Adolescents in the Art of Writing Well.* Newark, DE: International Reading Association.
Simon, S. B. (1972). *Values Clarification.* New York: Hart Publishing.

OUTCOMES

1. Students joined cooperative groups for the year.

2. I established a serious environment for writing.

3. Students wrote with sincerity and honesty.

4. I quickly learned the strengths and weaknesses of students as readers and writers.

5. Students realized that I would make their lives miserable if they misbehaved or were apathetic, so they decided to see what it felt like to give genuine effort.

ACTIVITIES

1. Communicate my high expectations for their performance and behavior in class.

2. Read letters from previous students.

3. Get a sample of students' writing. Have students do the assignment "creating man."

4. Read student compositions aloud. Read them for content, but note individual strengths and weaknesses.

5. Purposefully and carefully place students in groups. Appoint group leaders.

6. Go over policies for group work (emphasize how the individual is assessed within the group).

7. Introduce the World War III nuclear fallout exercise and writing assignment.

8. Have students describe a house from three different (emotional) perspectives without mentioning the emotion.

9. Read compositions aloud.

10. Conduct class outside; have students make lists of pivotal moments in their lives.

11. Have students write reflective essays about one particularly strong memory.

12. Go over peer critiquing. Allow no fluff, but encourage constructive, sincere feedback. Lean on the group leaders to be useful to other members in their group.

13. Have students revise, then read the reflective essays aloud.

14. Assess the reflective essays.

15. Speak to students individually about ways to enhance the quality of their writing.

2 Growing Up

Using students' childhood experiences to explore sixteen different kinds of writing

TIME: Three weeks

The Genesis for "Growing Up"

Matt Buzzard had the reputation as one of the worst behavior problems at school. A long list of special education labels—ADD (attention deficit disorder), ADHD (attention deficit hyperactivity disorder), ED (emotionally disturbed)—attempted to offer some rationale for Buzzard's continually aberrant behavior. Many teachers at school were afraid of him—a tall, muscular, audacious eighth grader who strutted around the hallways like he owned them, who talked and fidgeted constantly, who seemed to do what he wanted regardless of threats of reprisals. The first day of in-service before school, Matt Buzzard's seventh-grade English teacher came into my room as I was getting it ready for the first day of class.

"You've got him this year, thank God," she said with a huff.

"Got who?"

"You've got psycho Matt Buzzard in your second-period English class."

I asked her not to tell me any more. I didn't like hearing the gossip and former escapades of students before I had them in class. I think students deserve a fresh start every term. It's not like adolescence is a time when all your actions are rational and meticulously planned out. Still, I must admit that Buzzard's reputation had me a little worried.

"He's just plain psycho, that's all. You need to know that going in," she said. "Baines, I feel for you. I really do. Just get yourself a set of handcuffs and a muzzle and tie him to a post in the very back of the room."

From the first day of class, Buzzard was all that I had feared and more. Besides being irascible and unreasonable, he was fond of making abrupt airplane noises and knocking the books and papers of his classmates off their desks onto the floor. Many a time after I had worked hard to get the class launched on an assignment, out of nowhere Buzzard would scream, "BRRR . . . 747 about to crash . . . BRRRR . . . " Despite his outrageous behavior, I also noticed that he had an impressive vocabulary and would bring books to class so that he could surreptitiously read while everyone else worked on the day's activities, which he considered beneath him.

During the first few weeks of school, I had several one-on-one chats with Buzzard in which I tried to gently suggest that he tone down his antics. "I don't want to have to call your parents, Matt," I'd warn.

"Go ahead and call them, I don't care," Buzzard would answer.

So, I called his mom.

"What do you want me to do?" the mom asked. "You're the teacher. You're supposed to be the big expert on children. I mean, you're getting paid to work with Matt, so work with him."

When I saw Buzzard the next day, he said, "Hey dude. I heard that you called the house. Don't worry about it, man. My mom, she's not that pissed off at you . . . *yet.*" So much for the parent angle.

Next, I tried a performance contract that outlined precise consequences for Buzzard's misbehavior. First time, a warning. Second time, detention hall. Third time, to Assistant Principal Garza's office and a likely sentence of in-school suspension. Soon, I acquired the signatures of Buzzard, Garza and the other assistant principals, the principal, and even Buzzard's mom and filed the document in my drawer at school. Buzzard's behavior didn't change an iota. Every time Buzzard would misbehave, I would bring out the contract, state the rule, how he broke the rule, and go over the consequences. Soon, the procedure became predictable and I began to react to Buzzard's frequent outbursts perfunctorily, as if I were getting bored with the whole routine. And I was.

Buzzard would get two or three call-downs on Monday, serve a d-hall on Tuesday morning, then act like an idiot in class Tuesday afternoon, and get three days of in-house suspension for Wednesday, Thursday, and Friday. When attending in-house, I would send him work and he would complete most of it, though he would always manage to stamp his personality on every assignment. For example, when I asked for an informative description about a place he loved, most students turned in papers about their rooms at home or a favorite vacation spot, but Buzzard wrote a macabre description of a pork processing plant. When I asked for a composition from the perspective of a bird, Matt wrote yet another violent, bloody paper. Below, I offer two samples of the "bird" paper—one by Lisa, a "good student," and a second by Buzzard, who completed the assignment while relegated to the little, separate portable building that functioned as in-house suspension headquarters. I show these two works back-to-back to give you an idea of the singularity of Buzzard's vision.

A View from Above
by Lisa Beale

I feel myself lifting in the sky as a smoggy fist pushes me up. Looking down, I can see the tops of skyscrapers and the bottomless smoky pits of smokestacks. I can barely hear the otherwise deafening sounds of traffic as cars crawl along the wheel-like highway system far below me. It is all so repulsive, so unnatural.

As air carries me along further and further, the city pans out, leaving only the gold of the wilderness. A few cabins dot the wild country, as do a few small communities here and there. The pure air fills my tiny lungs and makes no effort to move me. The red dirt marks a small country road, winding throughout the pines and sycamores. Scenes of broad fields of wild grasses greet my straining eyes, and to my delight, they are filled with mice. I have reached the breeding and hunting grounds of my ancestors. I see many fields separated only by the sparse clusters of mesquite. This is true freedom, constantly threatened by the ever present destructive forces of man's evolution.

Because Lisa's paper had some good description—"sparse clusters of mesquite"—and some good sentence variety, her paper earned an A.

Spiral of Feathers
by Matt Buzzard

The rush of wind against my ears makes a violent sucking sound as I pick up speed and thrash side to side to throw off the aim of hunters below. I begin to slow down as a grove of trees becomes closer and closer. I descend towards a branch jutting out from a tree.

A shot rings out from the ground and I pull up higher and higher until the grove is nothing more than a dot on the ground. A bright field of green is now below me with dots of yellow littering the ground while raccoons scurry about feasting on what must be corn. I again start my way down circling until the ground looms closer.

Suddenly, a shot rings out sending a surge of pain through me. I begin to fall slowly as another shot rings out sending more hot streaks of fire through me.

The ground draws closer, I cannot move my wings, and I crash, smashing my face into the dirt. Blackness, a hand reaching toward my head and twisting. Crack.

Although it's a little on the gory side, Buzzard's composition displayed an atypical vocabulary for an eighth grader—*thrash, jutting, scurry, feasting, looms*—

and an interesting fragment—"Blackness, a hand reaching toward my head and twisting." Buzzard earned an A.

Over time, Buzzard's compositions began to get more and more graphic and he added another unique feature—every plot described novel ways that he could kill me. When I spoke to Buzzard about the latest trend in his writing, he seemed to become animated, even enthusiastic.

"What do you think, Baines? Some pretty good description in there, huh?"

Despite the gore and the troubling subject matter, Buzzard's compositions were pretty good. The ways that he could pervert the writing assignment so that he could "off" me in increasingly innovative ways showed a great deal of creativity and wit. When I asked the class to rewrite some common tales and fables to fit with contemporary times, Matt produced "Blood and Guts."

Blood and Guts
by Matt Buzzard

When the wolf was far out of sight, the horribly good girl hauled her horribly good butt full speed all the way home. She burst into the house causing quite a ruckus. As she ripped open the door of the dad's closet, she heard the noise of metal medals clanging. She slid back the bolt on the uzi 9 m.m. and locked the grenades onto her belt. Then, she was on her way to the park.

She quietly searched the park for the stupid prince who brought her here, the stupid pigs who the wolf was after, and the ugly mutated scum-sucking wolf. Suddenly, they were all running toward her, the pigs in the lead, with the prince and the wolf close behind. She flipped off the safety of her uzi 9 m.m. and let loose, mutilating the prince's innards.

"What are innards?" asked the littlest of the little mutants.

"Shut up," said the bachelor as he continued with the stupid story.

[An aside—I was a bachelor at this time in my life and I was fond of reading excerpts of good writing aloud. In this story, the bachelor was Baines.]

"Don't tell that little mutant to shut up," said the horribly good girl and she grabbed the hand of the littlest mutant and walked her safely away. Then she tossed two grenades down the shirt of the lonely bachelor and never showed up again in one of his stupid stories.

No one ever lives happily ever after.

Of course, with a different kind of student, I might have let the hysteria over school violence influence me. I could have responded with a severe reprimand, a serious talk with the principal, a recommendation to the school counselor (who had already told me in private, "Buzzard's a lost case"), and possibly a call to the police department. But, after our frequent run-ins, I had come to develop a weird, but genuine rapport with my tormentor. Despite the tough exterior, I had deduced that Buzzard was a very bright student with a mother who could not rein him in, enrolled in classes in which he felt continually stultified. Undoubtedly, he expected me to react to his outlandish compositions by trying to get him tossed out of school. Instead, I corrected errors, made some comments about the structure of his plot ("You should make it clear from the beginning that there are two realities—that of the good girl and that of the brilliant, good-looking bachelor"), and handed back his paper.

After a few weeks of compositions in which Buzzard showed increasing ingenuity at killing me, I wrote to him, "As much as I have come to enjoy reading about the torture and untimely death of this English teacher, I think the time has come to move on to a new subject. This one has grown a little tiresome."

I tried to think up some activities that would keep Buzzard interested enough that he wouldn't have the time or inclination to murder me again. I wanted to motivate not only Buzzard, but also the 179 or so other students in the rest of my classes, all of whom seemed to be from very different backgrounds, with varied abilities and talents.

If I really wanted to get Buzzard and the rest of my students reading, writing, and thinking, I couldn't very well go with the standard curriculum of "recommended literary works" and blah-blah state-issue objectives. Although that would have made my principal happy (at least for the moment), it would have forced Buzzard back on the warpath and put everyone else to sleep. While it is useful to know what is involved in the state assessment, any teacher who is worth a damn does not allow the state mandate du jour to dictate what happens in the sacred space of the classroom. To teach naked, I needed to formulate an approach that would genuinely engage students in the art of writing well. I wanted all my students (even Buzzard—heck, *especially* Buzzard) to write compositions of rare insight and beauty. And I wanted them to learn to love to write.

I don't see how anyone teaches writing without knowing exactly what each student is capable of doing, his or her weaknesses and strengths (spelling, sentence variety, vocabulary), interests (cheerleading, sports, music), sensitivity (how well do they accept criticism?), and tendencies (lazy, hard-working, obsessed with self-image, dogged by parents). As I thought about topics that might appeal to the very diverse students in my classes, I decided that the only trait they had in common was that they were adolescents who had somehow managed to make it to eighth grade. Some spoke Spanish at home, some had parents on the board at the country club, some were foster kids temporarily living with local families. I needed a grand plan, a map to help direct students where I wanted them to go. I wanted a plan that would not only ward off chaos, but one that would provide me with a plan of action for Monday morning and would serve me well in case the principal called me on the carpet. Oh yes, what was I trying to achieve? I wanted students to become accomplished, fearless writers. I wanted students to *want* to become accomplished, fearless writers.

I reread James Kinneavy's classic *A Theory of Discourse* (1971), one of the foundation texts upon which most assessments of writing for the past thirty years (including the writing portion of the National Assessment of Educational Progress and most state assessments) have been based. I also consulted several books on writing, such as Lawrence Block's *Writing the Novel* (1985), John Gardner's *The Art of Fiction* (1985), Anne Lamott's *Bird by Bird* (1995), and Kirby, Liner, and Vinz's *Inside Out* (1988). Then I started trying to conjure up ways to engage students in an experience that would keep them writing, writing, writing until the world ran out of ink (or ink cartridges for the printer, anyway).

A Framework for Writing: Aim and Mode

Kinneavy classified the major aims of writing as expressive, persuasive, referential, and literary. Venting over something you find irritating or scribbling in a diary how you feel around that someone special would constitute an expressive aim. In a persuasive paper, the writer attempts to influence the reader toward a certain point of view. A common example is an editorial in a newspaper. Although Kinneavy labeled the third aim as *referential*, it may be easier to think of it as *informative*, where the goal of the writer is to enlighten the reader on a certain topic. Most textbooks and objective renderings of news stories are written with an informative or referential purpose. Fourth, a writer may have a literary goal, that is, the writer may want to create an aesthetic experience for the reader. Such an author might choose any number of vehicles—poetry (ballad, haiku, limerick), short story, novel, Web page, script, or play—to satisfy this literary impulse. Table 2.1 offers examples of activities for each different aim of writing.

The second consideration is the mode of writing. To satisfy a particular aim, a writer may choose any one of four major modes—description, narration, evaluation, or classification. An example of a descriptive mode is any passage from Charles Dickens or other Victorian novelist fond of describing settings in intricate detail. A narrative mode involves structuring a response so that it tells a story. Biographies, feature stories, and most novels are organized around a story. In an evaluation mode, the writer's purpose is to assess the strengths and weaknesses of a particular experience, person, or place. The comparison/contrast assignment, found in most writing textbooks, qualifies as an evaluative paper.

TABLE 2.1   The Aims of Writing

Aim	Examples
Expressive	Journal, "shotgun" piece of writing that describes a current emotional state
Persuasive	Political speech, newspaper editorial
Informative	Textbook, brochure that describes the symptoms of the chicken pox
Literary	*Fences,* "Love Song of J. Alfred Prufrock," *Of Mice and Men,* "Hills Like White Elephants"

Finally, the classification mode is an academic paper in which the writer provides the reader with some sort of organizing system that can enhance understanding of events or objects. Anthropologists frequently use the classificatory mode, as they categorize artifacts as being from a specific time period or a particular region of the world. Examples of the different modes of writing are explicated in Table 2.2.

Okay, okay, I know what you're thinking. "Baines, enough already with this technical mumbo-jumbo; cut to the chase, partner." Here's the punchline. Four aims and four modes produce sixteen very different kinds of writing assignments (see Table 2.3). The big breakthrough for me was realizing that I didn't have to get bogged down in only one kind of assignment. Those budding short story writers could rip out a literary narrative, and my future accountants might write an informative description. For me, the matrix was a useful reminder not to get into a rut in the kinds of assignments I asked of students.

In designing the activities for the "Growing Up" project, I concocted writing assignments that fit Kinneavy's models and threw in some multimedia experiences that I thought students would find challenging and relevant.

So, here's hoping you don't make Kinneavy's matrix another form of drudgery, but that you use it as a reminder to give students a chance to play with a variety of different kinds of writing. It's also useful to have students cite a specific audience now and then. It might make a difference in style and word choice if prospective readers were seven or seventy-seven, male or female, academics or workers in a fast-food restaurant, teachers or peers.

TABLE 2.2   The Modes of Writing

Mode	Examples
Descriptive	Descriptions of settings or a character's physical appearance in novels, article describing an exotic locale in a travel magazine
Narrative	Biography, feature story, most novels
Evaluative	Comparison/contrast paper, article or book ranking U.S. presidents from best to worst, paper explaining which recent event has had the most deleterious effect on the American economy
Classificatory	Explanation of the NAEP Writing Assessment Scale (0–6), article in an anthropology magazine describing the time period of an artifact, doctor making a diagnosis based upon a patient's symptoms

TABLE 2.3   Kinneavy's Matrix (with a Twist)

	A. Description	B. Narration	C. Evaluation	D. Classification
1. *Expressive*	**1A.** Describe something—a photograph, an incident, an object—from two perspectives—a parent, friend, sibling, teacher, or neighbor. Use the same point of view for both (either first or third person).	**1B.** Write a story (a) expressing how you felt after you lost a beloved pet (b) explaining how you felt after a big event in your life, or (c) describing your thoughts and actions in a typical day as a child.	**1C.** Look at a series of works of art, then explain which work best symbolizes what life was like for you growing up. Explain.	**1D.** When you ponder the whole of your childhood, what kinds of feelings are elicited? Can you categorize the events of your childhood into constructive and destructive? Normal or abnormal? What kind of categorization makes the most sense? Why?
2. *Persuasive*	**2A.** Through a description of yourself from a third-person perspective, convince the reader that you are brilliant and good-looking (or any combination of traits).	**2B.** Write a seemingly objective story involving someone you knew well (but didn't like) as a child. Although the person might be evil or apathetic, attempt to portray him/her sympathetically.	**2C.** Write an essay in which you compare and contrast the advantages of growing up. Persuade the reader that growing up is either fun and positive or boring and negative (or some other combination).	**2D.** Looking back, do events that happened to you as a child now seem preordained or were they arbitrary? Is life better classified as a fulfillment of destiny or a trip into uncharted waters?
3. *Informative*	**3A.1.** Describe your top eight fears as a child. **3A.2.** Describe your top ten thrills as a child. **3A.3.** Describe a possession that was significant to you as a child. Describe it so thoroughly that a reader could pick it out of a thousand items.	**3B.** Draw a map of the neighborhood in which you lived as a child. Then, tell a story that includes the different areas—the places where you played, the forbidden zones, etc.	**3C.** Describe the hardest thing about growing up.	**3D.1.** List ten activities you could do as a child that you can't do now. **3D.2.** List ten activities you do now that you could not do as a child. **3D.3.** Write an essay on what constitutes adolescence, childhood, adulthood, or similar topic.

TABLE 2.3   *continued*

	A. Description	B. Narration	C. Evaluation	D. Classification
4. *Literary*	**4A.** Write a poem or short story that describes in detail someone you felt strongly about as a child. Find sets of images that represent lines of the poem or sections of the story. Capture the images on the Internet or scan them from magazines. Insert the images into a PowerPoint presentation. Then, play the PowerPoint poem or story as you read the poem or story aloud.	**4B.** Write a short story in which you describe an interaction between two characters from your childhood (not yourself). Write a dialogue in which each person is trying to hide a secret from the other. Do not openly reveal the secrets, but make the reader discover them through indirect description and innuendo.	**4C.** Write a screenplay that addresses the complexities of an issue that was of particular interest to you as a child—staying up all night, moving to a new neighborhood or school, playing sports, friends, etc. Film it.	**4D.** Write an academic essay differentiating between relaxing and goofing off; cool and uncool; a child and an adult; schooling and education; living and going through the motions.

Even in our plug-in age, most teachers still require students to write for an audience of one—the teacher as evaluator (see James Britton et al., 1975, for a lengthy academic discussion on audience). Other audiences might include the teacher as editor (one who edits and comments, but doesn't give a grade), peers as editors (the traditional writing project formula), peers as readers, younger audiences, older audiences, general mass appeal, literary contest, self, self and close friends, newspaper, magazine, random Web surfers, directed Web surfers, state composition evaluators, or conference participants (writer's forum, presentation days, etc.). For the "Growing Up" project, I asked students to write for prospective book publishers, the teacher as editor (so that they would abide by conventions of spelling and grammar), and fellow adolescents. Still, students could list who they wanted as the audience. A female student once said that she wanted to direct her work toward her many relatives in Eastern Europe who were curious about American life. The girl worked as hard as any student I've ever had in attempting to create meaningful, heartfelt, grammatically perfect papers.

For any of the sixteen assignments listed in the Kinneavy matrix, I always left open the option of medium—composing a poem (preferably in a specific format, such as a sonnet), writing a play or essay, shooting a video, or creating a Web page.

I guarantee that whatever mode of writing the state says it is looking for this year will not be the same as the one it wants next year. However, the Kinneavy matrix pretty much has them all covered. The important thing about teaching writing is that students learn to write with poise and (this is tough) understated eloquence. If you are worth your salt as a teacher, you'll learn your students' talents and you'll follow your hunches.

One day after a shocking shooting at a local school, I posed the question, "Is it ever justifiable to kill another human being? If you had had the chance and the moment presented itself, would you have killed Hitler? McVeigh?" After some heated discussion among students, I asked them to write out their position on the taking of a human life.

Only later did I realize that I had asked students to compose a persuasive–classifactory piece of writing. At the top of his paper (in which he advocated eliminating not only Hitler and McVeigh, but a litany of serial killers and terrorists), Buzzard wrote: "To the audience of my very depressed teacher. To arms, Baines, to arms!"

For the "growing up" experience, I asked students to keep all handouts, lists, rough drafts, and final papers in one notebook, which they turned in at the end of the project. I gave students one "big grade" on their final written product and another smaller grade for all the work they did leading up to it (evident in the notebook).

Sequence of Activities

Day 1: Getting to Know the Child Within

"What were you like as a kid?" I asked.

That question prompted at least a few smiles and several spontaneous responses.

"Goofy."

"I was a beautiful baby."

"I used to lick the outsides of gumball machines."

To give students a "feel" for writing about childhood, I read a few funny excerpts from Christopher Curtis's *The Watsons Go to Birmingham 1963* (1995) and Gary Paulsen's *Harris and Me* (1995). I asked students to focus upon an age that they remembered vividly.

"Get out a sheet of paper. Write down the year of your life you would like to write about along with the names of family members, the town where you lived, and any other details that you can recall. Blurt it all out on paper right now as it comes to you."

I kept quiet for ten minutes and let students write. When it seemed like everyone was done, I asked, "Who wasn't born in Georgia?"

Janna raised her hand and explained that she had been born in Boston and lived with her grandmother in a small apartment until she was two. Then they moved back to Georgia. But after her parents divorced, she returned to Boston and lived there for two years before moving back to Georgia for good. The second stint in Boston, when she was five and six, were the years she wanted to write about because, she said, "My grandma was crazy!" Since I had a pull-down map of the United States in the room, I asked Janna to point out Boston for everyone in class.

Manny said he was born in Nuevo Laredo, "the armpit of the world, man. I mean, you look forward to dust storms. That's the highlight." Manny pointed out the border town of Nuevo Laredo on the map as well.

Buzzard insisted that his mom kept him in the cupboard when he was a baby. "I was in there with the pots and pans."

As students discussed aspects of their childhood, I asked questions as a talk show host might. Eventually, I tried to steer the conversation toward childhood fears, monsters under the bed, bogeymen in the closet, nightmares, and dreams. Then I asked them to write out eight of their biggest fears as children. After a few minutes of mad scribbling, I asked students to read some of their lists. I wrote most of their comments on the board until it was filled up with darkness, vampires, vicious dogs, snakes, bullies, ticks, poison ivy, Jason, Freddie Krueger, and black widow spiders. Surprisingly, the most common fear among my eighth graders was abandonment.

To close the class on a positive note, I asked students to list their top ten thrills of childhood. "You know, did you enjoy the roller coaster at Six Flags? Did you like playing with dolls? Did you meet a really good friend? Did you win any contests for art or music?"

"Happy meals at McDonald's."

"Playing hide and seek after dark with flashlights."

"Hanging out with my dad" (from Buzzard).

Finally, I handed out the evaluation sheet for the final elaboration (see Table 2.4). "This is what you'll be graded on eventually. For right now, just look it over, see the kinds of things that I'll be looking for, and get it out when you've decided to begin the final elaboration."

"When do we begin writing it?"

"Whenever you feel like it. It is not due for a few weeks, but you should probably think about what you might want to do. That way, you can work on it when you get a few minutes here and there."

Day 2: Changing Perspectives

At the beginning of class, I highlighted some stories we had heard the previous day.

"Hey, anybody remember where Manny was born? Anyone remember Buzzard's greatest thrill as a kid?" After students began talking about some of the tidbits we learned about each other the day before, I asked, "You know, when you are a little kid, you probably loved having your parents lie down with you in bed at night. But you might not be as enthusiastic about such a prospect these days, eh?"

Students laughed.

TABLE 2.4   Final Elaboration Evaluation Sheet

Choose one of the 6 options below:

1. Write a poem or short story that describes in detail someone you felt strongly about as a child. Find sets of images that represent lines of the poem or sections of the story. Capture the images on the Internet or scan them from magazines. Insert the images into a PowerPoint presentation. Then, play the Power-Point poem or story as you read the poem or story aloud.

2. Write a short story in which you describe an interaction between two characters from your childhood (not yourself). Write a dialogue in which each person is trying to hide a secret from the other. Do not openly reveal the secrets, but make the reader discover them through indirect description and innuendo.

3. Write a screenplay that addresses the complexities of an issue that was of particular interest to you as a child—staying up all night, moving to a new neighborhood or school, playing sports, etc. Film it.

4. Write an academic essay differentiating between relaxing and goofing off; cool and uncool; a child and an adult; schooling and education; living and going through the motions.

5. Choose any single assignment from the "growing up" experience and expand upon it.

6. Create a composition in which you synthesize aspects from several or all of your writing assignments.

Grading scale:
1. Ability to capture the reader's interest (20 points)
2. Choice of words, control of the language (20 points)
3. Awareness of audience (20 points)
4. Appropriate language conventions (spelling, capitalization, punctuation, grammar) (20 points)
5. Ideas, organization, and clarity (20 points)

Two strengths of your final elaboration were:

_____

_____

Two weaknesses of your final elaboration were:

_____

_____

Overall grade: _____

"Hey, I used to think my old elementary school was huge, but when I went back last year, the halls were so small, I couldn't believe it. I was taller than most of the teachers."

"I used to think I was cool when I got to wear these red plastic rain boots. Now, they would be pretty embarrassing."

"I used to think N Sync were the best. I mean, I had all these posters on my walls and I bought all their albums. Now I think, 'Who are these short guys with all this hairspray?'"

When the conversation began to falter, I asked students to write a new list: "Nine things I could do as a child that I can't get away with now." They seemed to like this one. When they finished, many students actually volunteered to read their responses aloud.

"Peeing the bed."

"You can't cry every time you don't get your way."

"Back then, when I made funny noises, everyone said it was cute. Now my mom says I'm gross."

Next, I asked students to write "Ten things I can do as an adolescent that I couldn't do as a child." This was more serious stuff. After a few more minutes of thinking and writing, students shared these lists, too.

"Watch R-rated movies."

"Go out on a date."

"Wear makeup."

"Go places without your parents."

Because I felt like I had some momentum going, I asked students to try a more lengthy assignment. "Now I want you to describe something—an event, an incident, a photograph, an object—from two perspectives, one from your perspective as a kid and another as you see it now [expressive–descriptive]. But, you have to keep your perspective consistent. Also, make it interesting to read and reflective of how you really felt."

Manny seemed to connect with the assignment.

Useless Space (fourth grade)
by Manny Valdez

Lying in the dark shadows of the night, I looked up towards the sky that trapped and enclosed me. The silent trees seemed to be closing in on me, to bend over and observe me. Above was space, useless space, with no purpose or meaning. Scattered among the dark space were stars. Stars of hot, scorching, radiant energy. On these stars were constant explosions of nuclear friction, blazing light across the vast space, the space which contains our world of colors that will soon fade away.

Wonders of the Night (now)
by Manny Valdez

The midnight sky was full of romance. The never ending horizon reminded me that there were no limits on my possibilities—they were infinite. The bright moon was mysterious, filled with wonder, wonder of what lies beyond, the wonder of what the future holds for me. What great things are to become of this world, when fantasy and imagination become real, events occurring beyond our dreams. The flourishing plants and trees surrounding me as I gazed at the sky were full of life. The stars were like twinkles in the eyes of someone you trust.

When I first read his paper, it was difficult for me to believe that Manny's conception of the night sky as a fourth grader was grounded in existentialist angst and the big bang. However, Manny said that when he was in fourth grade, he was obsessed with the solar system. Once, he saw a short film about space and he learned that the universe was constantly changing—expanding and contracting, and planets were constantly dying and being born. Manny had interpreted the film to mean that earth, like any planet in the universe, could blow up and disappear at any moment. Apparently the idea stayed with him for years. It still seemed to scare him a little.

Manny's paper was a success for a number of reasons, most notably because he managed to convey completely different descriptions of the same phenomenon (the night sky) and he seemed "invested" in the quality of his work—a first for Manny, at least in my class.

Days 3 and 4: Music and Images of Childhood

When I begin a new project, I like to overlap due dates. For example, on Monday, I assigned the "objects from two perspectives" paper and set its due date for Thursday. On Wednesday, I planned to assign another writing assignment due the following Tuesday. An advantage to rotating deadlines is that papers trickle in over time rather than flood in all at once. A second advantage is that students have a choice among assignments on which they can work.

When I assign compositions for a grade, I encourage students to turn them in for my comments before the due date. For many writing assignments, I give students a check to indicate that they have successfully completed it. However, I still write all over student papers: "I laughed out loud when I read about the burping contests with your brother"; "I don't understand what you mean"; "Great sentence!" On their papers and in our face-to-face conversations about writing, I respond to students authentically, writer-to-writer. When it comes time to evaluate a student's paper for a grade, I have already read so many of their papers and conferred with them so often that I feel quite comfortable in assigning a grade. Students seem comfortable with it, too.

Students know that I will sometimes demand that an assignment be rewritten when the situation warrants—when the composition represents little or no effort, when it's on the verge of greatness but just needs a little work, or when the composition contains numerous repetitive or egregious errors. I will not give a student credit for an assignment until he or she has done it to my satisfaction.

The major part of the grade for the "growing up" experience is derived from the "final elaboration," which is due towards the end of the experience, but I encourage students to work on it whenever they get a free minute. When I feel the need to record a grade, I tell students, "This is for a grade" at the time I make the assignment and immediately hand out a rubric for evaluation. Then I go over the rubric step-by-step so students know how their work will be graded. I build the assessment for a composition based upon what I want students to learn at the time.

For example, if I am concerned that students learn how to write and punctuate dialogue, I may weigh that component more heavily than others. Just between you and me, I confess that, in spite of any fancy-looking rubrics, I still tend to grade holistically. I begin grading by thinking, "This is a B paper." Then, if the paper goes beyond my expectations, it may earn an A. If the paper does not live up to expectations, it earns a grade lower than a B. After I determine what grade a paper deserves, I go to the rubric to help me justify it and to communicate to the student the specific area in which the composition needs work. With every piece of writing, no matter how good or bad, I always point out something positive and something that could be improved upon.

For the final elaboration, students may choose among a variety of topics. Because the assignments build upon one another, students should not attempt to rush the "final elaboration," but let ideas jell in their heads as they complete the lead-up activities. Although I grade for quality, not length, students have turned in ninety-page novels, ninety-minute videos, and ninety-slide PowerPoint presentations. I have also had a student create a single-page poem as a "final elaboration." I want students to create works of eloquence and style. I'm loose about length.

After students completed a modicum of writing on their childhood, I brought in a few musical selections about childhood. From classical music, I selected something from Robert Schumann's *Scenes from Childhood.* I am particularly fond of Schumann's short piece from this work called "Traumerei." Next, I played Claude Debussy's "Reverie" and "Clair de Lune." After each piece of music, I asked students to write out what they thought the composer was communicating about childhood. When I asked students what piece of music (popular or classical) would best represent their childhood thus far, Manny said, "Something that is really loud and fast."

Buzzard said, "Bad to the Bone."

Janna said, "Clair de Lune."

On the fourth day, I brought in several posters, art books, books on photography, postcards, and several downloaded images from the Internet. (Museum sites and commercial publishers with free images such as pdimages.com are good sources for images.) Then I passed them around and asked students to select an image that best symbolized their childhood. If they could not find a suitable image among the resources I furnished, they could use a photograph from home or could draw, paint, or sculpt an original work. For students who chose the latter option, I encouraged abstract and weird creations (that way, they would have to write more to explain what they had created).

Once everyone found or created an image that represented their childhood, I asked students to write an essay describing why and how the image they selected or created represented their childhood. (For those of you checking off boxes on the Kinneavy Matrix, this would constitute an informative–descriptive assignment, though students often turned it into an expressive–narrative). Janna chose the painting *Journey of the Butterfly* by Salvador Dali.

How Dali's *Paysage aux Papillons* Relates to My Childhood
by Janna Leonard

Butterflies. Probably one of the most magnificent creatures on earth. I felt like I was one when I took dance and was up on the stage. I loved dance for the 11 years of my life I devoted to it. People loved me, too. I was my dance teacher's favorite—I was her substitute teacher and I was the only student she ever let choreograph for the recitals, and I was damn good at that, too.

Why does my life as a dancer relate to Dali's *Paysage aux Papillons*? Because, people always stop to look at butterflies as they dance across the air, just as people remembered me after I had been on stage. I could feel it, electrifying, one of the biggest rushes I've ever had. I could do it all—tap, jazz, modern, ballet—and more, and I did all of it well. It was a feeling like flying or floating. Like the butterflies in the picture I was graceful, but in the picture they seem to be flying away—out of view. So was I.

I never danced again after my last recital in Columbus, GA. All of the competition award ribbons and plaques and all of the recital bouquets dried in vases in my room are the reminders I have of those days. I felt it was time to grow up, and to put away my dancing shoes. Why I equated being a dancer with being a little girl I have never been able to understand, but it made sense at the time. Perhaps it was because I had finally proved to myself that I was awesome at something, so maybe I thought I didn't need to dance anymore. So, I quit . . . and I have never, ever regretting doing something so much as that.

When everyone was finished, one student would read his/her composition aloud while a friend walked around the room slowly carrying the image, so that the class could get a good look.

Day 5: Reviving Show and Tell

At the end of the first week, I planned a show and tell. During the show and tell, students would bring in a significant childhood possession and explain why it was important. Because pets played such a crucial role in the lives of many of my students, I let pets serve as significant childhood possessions, too (though I requested that students not bring their pets to show and tell). I asked students to either (1) write a story involving their most treasured possession, which could include pets (narrative–informative) or (2) write a description of the object (or pet) so that the reader would implicitly understand and appreciate the object's significance (descriptive–persuasive). Students showed off their most treasured possessions and read their papers in a kind of low-key show and tell.

Lately, Manny had started responding to several prompts by writing about his deceased cat Sugums, whom he apparently loved very much. When he got the opportunity to write about Sugums's death, he wrote a serious, stirring twelve-page tribute. To spare you, oh gentle reader, I will include here only three brief paragraphs from Manny's tome.

Sugums
by Manny Valdez

. . . The most shocking thing that ever happened at the serene location I call home was the brutal accidental killing of the family cat, Sugums. Sugums was a fighter as she had been all her life. Even at the ripe old age of 10 (70 in cat years) she could still completely knock the stuffing out of any cat on our block. I loved Sugums. I couldn't remember the time she almost scratched one of my eyes. I had been too young when it happened. She had seen it all . . . the mother of a splendid litter of kittens, all of whom, save one, had run off to seek their fortunes. She had once beaten up a Great Dane dog, even bigger than I was and almost five times as big as Sugums, for coming too close to her kittens. A calico cat, tan, black and white with deadly sharp claws and a deceptive "baby face," she had become as much a part of my life as eating. She had been with my parents longer than I had been. . . .

. . . To someone who has never had a pet, a dead cat would not be such a big deal. But I was crushed. An aspect of my life that had been with me as long as I could remember was gone, done in, never to return. It had only taken reality three short seconds to change my entire life. . . . I held Copper Puppy close to me. Copper was such a good stuffed friend. I seemed to feel security flowing into me from his soft yellow fur. From his long, floppy, fuzzy brown ears to his loosely stitched little tail to his chubby stuffed cheeks, he was a symbol of comfort to me. The darkness dispersed, the monster was vanquished, and the face disappeared from the window. . . . Coming into contact with an object that reminds one of life before a change, helps one recover from the pain. . . .

Days 6 and 7: Mapping Out the Old Neighborhood

In the first ten to fifteen minutes of the film *Stand by Me* (after the credits), all the main characters are introduced. Before I showed the clip, I asked students to note the quality of the dialogue. After I played the clip, I asked, "Is it a fair representation of how kids speak?"

The class discussed the extent to which the writers (screenwriters Raynold Gideon and Bruce A. Evans, who translated Steven King's novella for film) captured the rhythm and give-and-take of real conversation.

I asked, "Do any of the characters from the film remind you of anyone you know? Do any characters talk funny? Do any have distinctive characteristics? How did the writers communicate these characteristics—through action, dialogue, setting?"

After students gave a so-so rating to the dialogue of *Stand by Me,* I asked about the neighborhoods where they grew up. "Tell me about the kind eighty-year-olds, the mean kids, your best friends, haunted houses, the places that were the most fun, areas that were off-limits." Students were eager to share the stories, myths, and legends from their neighborhood, and there were many neighborhoods represented in class.

After a few minutes of trading stories, I read aloud a description of a neighborhood from Robert Lipsyte's *The Contender.*

> He waited on the stoop until twilight, pretending to watch the sun melt into the dirty gray Harlem sky. Up and down the street transistor radios clicked on and hummed into the sour air. Men dragged out card tables, laughing. Cars cruised through the garbage and broken glass, older guys showing off their Friday night girls. . . . (1967, p. 1).

Then, I read from Stephen Crane's "The Blue Hotel."

> The Palace Hotel at Fort Romper was painted a light blue, a shade that is on the legs of a kind of heron, causing the bird to declare its position against any background. The Palace Hotel, then, was always screaming and howling in a way that made the dazzling winter landscape of Nebraska seem only a grey swampish hush. It stood alone on the prairie, and when the snow was falling the town two hundred yards away was not visible. . . . (1955, p. 286).

I handed two blank, white sheets of paper to each student. "On one paper, draw a map of the neighborhood where you grew up. Include as much detail on the map as possible—best friend's house, bully's house, danger zone, playground, store, school. Janna, you should note all the places that you and your crazy grandmother used to go around the neighborhood in Boston. On the other sheet, write out an explanation for your map."

After students drew maps, they wrote (a) a description of the neighborhood or (b) a story that included vivid descriptions of the neighborhood. Then I put students into groups of three or four. Once everyone was finished writing, they shared their maps and stories with other members of their group.

Manny chose to write a description, rather than a story. I liked Manny's paper because he wrote with clarity in a completely natural voice. As with the lists of fears, thrills, freedoms, and limitations of childhood, the essay on the neighborhood provided much fodder for subsequent discussions. I have always found intense discussions to be a good catalyst for effective writing.

"My Neighborhood" was written by Manny (author of the twelve-pager on Sugums), a twelve-year-old, average student in an eighth-grade English class.

My Neighborhood
by Manny Valdez

I guess my neighborhood was a typical neighborhood, but then I wouldn't know—it's the only neighborhood I've ever known. My house is on the dead end circle of Lee Way, so if I couldn't cross the street it was always okay because I could just walk around the circle and end up on the other side. I lived in a one story normal sized brick house with gray siding. I lived with my parents, my three older sisters, and my dog. My best friend's name was Juan. I guess he was my best friend because he was the only little boy around, the only kid I remember playing with.

The thing I remember most about Juan is that when it was time for him to go home his dad would whistle for him like he was a dog. There was a little ugly girl across the street from Juan that I think he liked but I never could justify it. Next door to Juan was my babysitter who was a little lame-brained. She once put a metal pot in our microwave and blew it up. Another time she took me to a party and told me not to tell my parents. Right, like a seven-year-old kid wants to keep it a secret that he crashes a party of wild teenagers.

On the other side of the house was a strange man. All I remember is once he threw a wrench at my dog for urinating in his yard. Next to the dog-lover was a druggy kid, and on some nights when the breeze was just right, from my front porch, you could smell him smoking an endless stream of marijuana cigarettes. That house was a no-no! Next to the kid was a very nice lady that my mom used to go see, when she needed my mom (who is a nurse) to give her a shot in her butt. Sometimes I would go over to her house and pick strawberries from her patch. I learned the word *kumquat* from the people next to the shot lady, an old couple who liked to sit on their porch and watch everybody in the neighborhood. They always said they watched all my sisters grow up on that porch. They were always giving us fruits and stuff from their garden. Across the street was another nice old couple with a really fat cat, but not too long ago the woman died and the man moved, and some Salvadorans who can hardly speak any English live there now.

Anyway, back to my childhood. Somewhere in the neighborhood was a kid that never could leave his house. I could never figure out why he couldn't leave, or why his mom made him sit in the back seat of the car all the time, even when there was no one in the front, and why he had no friends. The mystery kid still lives in that house and I'm wondering what he looks like now and if he is some sickly kid with an incurable disease or something.

Days 8 and 9: Poetry and Pie Charts

I don't want you to forget about old Buzzard. After some initial squawking, he began participating fully. He loved talking and writing about his childhood, his life in the cupboard, his dad, and his crazy brothers. Not only did the body count and gross quotient decline rapidly, Buzzard made impressive strides as a writer. I would be showing off more of Buzzard's work at this point, but Buzzard managed to lose his notebook at the end of the grading period (after I graded it, thank goodness). Well, to be honest, Buzzard told me that aliens stole his notebook so that they could create a new race of worker slaves based upon his notes, but I just didn't believe him. So, I have none of Buzzard's interim assignments. Fortunately, I kept his final paper, which I'll share with you at the end of the chapter.

I felt like some poetry, so I began the day by reading two favorite poems about growing old, Shakespeare's Sonnet 60 ("Like as the waves make towards the pebbled shore, / So do our minutes hasten to their end") and Alfred, Lord Tennyson's "Break, Break, Break" ("Break break break, / At the foot of thy crags o sea, / But the tender grace of a day that is dead, / Will never come back to me").

I asked students what they thought of the poems. Then, I asked if any of them had arrived at an epiphany about childhood. Regarding childhood, Percy Shelley once wrote, "It is to have a spirit yet streaming from the waters of baptism; it is to believe in love, to believe in loveliness, to believe in belief" (in Lorie and Mascetti 1996, p. 30). I handed out copies of the poems by Tennyson and Shakespeare and asked students to write a mock poem (a poem written in the same format). Through the mock poem, I wanted students to depict an aspect of their childhood. For example, Alison began her poem, "Ache, ache, ache / o my little ear, o mom / I knew not your lungs could scream / such angry words at me. . . ." Some students added music or rhythm to their poems (beating on the desk, clapping, and stomping were how most students added rhythm) and those who wanted to performed them for the rest of class.

As a closing activity, I asked students how they spent a usual Saturday as a child. I asked them to draw a pie chart that represented the hours that they would have spent sleeping, eating, playing, reading, watching television, and doing other kinds of activities (team sports, practicing the piano, karate lessons, etc.) on a typical Saturday. Then I asked them to write a few paragraphs that helped explain the pie chart. Needless to say, television usually occupied more time than any other single activity on most charts.

Day 10: The Big One

At the beginning of class, I asked students to get out all their writing to date—pie chart, neighborhood map (with accompanying descriptions or stories), and other assignments. Then I said, "Write a story that describes (a) a typical day in your life as a child or (b) an important event in your childhood. This assignment will be for a grade." I wrote the two options on the board, handed out the grading rubric (see Table 2.5), and fielded questions.

After students finished their papers, I passed out two more copies of the grading scale. Then I asked students to read at least two compositions penned by other students and to evaluate them as I would. After peer editing, students returned the evaluations to the writer, who revised the paper and handed it in to me with the two peer evaluations.

TABLE 2.5   Narrative Writing Assessment

Assessment for "A Day in the Life" or "An Important Event"

Dialogue (realistic, punctuated correctly)	0	10	20
Clear, expressive language	0	10	20
Physical descriptions of setting, you, and friends	0	10	20
Vary sentence structure, spelling, grammar	0	10	20
Interesting plot	0	10	20

+ Comments:

_____

_____

_____

_____

Areas that need special attention:

_____

_____

_____

_____

Overall grade: _____

Some students described a wrenching move to a new house in a new city while others described some seemingly innocuous incident, such as finding a dead snake while playing with friends. It's funny what adolescents consider "an important event." Of course, Manny wrote another tribute to Sugums, this one a twenty-pager in which he wrote from the perspective of the cat. Although both of his peers were moved by his paper, they could not finish reading it during the allotted time. So, I made copies, which each took home to finish. Both students gave Manny some useful suggestions regarding use of language and dialogue, which he graciously heeded. The twenty-page dirge on Sugums was depressing, but it was also Manny's best paper yet.

Day 11: Chance and Destiny

I opened class by citing Joseph Campbell: "When you look back on your life, it looks as though it were a plot, but when you are into it, it's a mess: just one surprise after another. Then, later, you see it was perfect. So, I have a theory that if you are on your own path things are going to come to you" (1988, p. 63).

I asked students, "In your childhood, do you think you were on a path that magically opened up for you, or do you feel more like you were hacking your way through a jungle? I want you to write a persuasive paper to convince me of your belief in destiny or in the role of luck" (persuasive–classifactory).

Chance and Destiny
by Janna Leonard

It's a hard thing for someone to decide whether or not the events of their childhood were predestined things or if they were all due to chance. Overall, I'm pretty sure the things that happened during my childhood were basically going to happen, rather than arbitrary. My parents had a "bad idea" of a marriage from the very beginning. It wasn't going to last, and if they'd been a bit older before they had married, I think they would've realized that. My father was not a guy who was going to be a father, and I can't imagine him ever being such. His work was more important than family and even when my parents were married it seems like he was only with us once in a while, sometimes gone for almost a year at a time. So, I think that my brother and I were almost meant to have that kind of a childhood—the kind where your parents divorce, you lose touch with your father's family, your mother feels abandoned, you feel abandoned, etc.

But, I think we were also meant to be taken care of. In that, I'm referring to my grandparents. It wasn't like I never had a father figure. My grandfather was that and more, and he was a better one than my real dad could've been. And, my mom had her mom, my grandmother, to lean on through all the tough times that a divorce brings on.

It's sad to say, but as far as childhood goes, a lot of that is set out for a kid by the decisions their parents make. Things change as you grow up, though. After childhood is over and you become an adult you begin to choose your own path. Then things are more due to chance, but they can seem pre-ordained (boy and girl meet on a bus, they are on the same bus by chance, and therefore meet by chance, but they believe they were meant to meet).

Days 12 to 15: The Final Elaboration

By now, students should have finished all the revisions for previous assignments (I checked them off in their notebooks). Although students may have long ago begun their "final elaboration," all of us are guilty of waiting until the last minute at one time or another. During the last few days of the project, I try to make myself available to students should they wish to confer about their final elaborations. One beautiful aspect of the "Growing Up" project is that, by the end of it, most students have a large notebook full of writing, so selecting the final topic is more a matter of choosing among existing great ideas than thinking up something completely new.

Students put the final elaboration in the front of their project notebook so that, while I evaluate it, I can also see all their previous work, along with comments on earlier drafts and notes from their peers. On the grade sheet, I write at least two positive comments and make no more than two suggestions for improvement. I have found that if you exceed the rule of two for "suggestions for improvement," students' eyes glaze over and they begin to suspect that their work was an utter failure. Because I want them to keep writing, I am specific and brief. The final elaboration is a major grade representative of three weeks of work. I also give students a lesser grade (okay, an effort grade) for completing the assignments found in their notebooks.

So, here's the clincher on Matt Buzzard. Although he wrote a seventy-page novella as part of his notebook (which he lost to the aliens), he handed in a two-page short story for the final elaboration. In some descriptions of his neighborhood, Buzzard remembered an attractive young girl who had gotten pregnant and then disappeared, though her parents and a brother remained in the neighborhood. Buzzard selected assignment #2 for his final elaboration. He described an interaction between two persons in which each was attempting to hide something from the other (narrative–literary).

Secrets
by Matt Buzzard

It was beautiful, a blue dress laced with jewels and satin fringes. A dress worthy of royalty, and made for me. Maybe my mother decided she would forgive me for denying her marriage to another man. When father died, mom swore to never marry again, or to never have children of a different blood. Then she went and married that man who we all (my younger brother and sister twins) despised. So I yelled at her, cussed at her and screamed at her. Then, she went and bought me this ballerina dance dress.

I twirled and spun, pirouetted and jumped.

RR . . . RIP!

"Oh no!"

"Honey, please come down and show me your new dress," called my mother.

"Uh . . ." I stammered through a closed door. "I . . . um, well, I . . . "

"Come on, honey," she insisted.

I came through the door with my back away from her.

"Well," she said, "Let's see it."

"Mom, have you gained weight?" I said changing the subject.

"Oh, you mean this?" she said, patting her middle. "It's just honeymoon fat." She sort of looked at the floor.

"Mom, what's wrong?"

"Oh, nothing. It's just that . . . " she glanced at her stomach as I played with the back of my dress. "Anyway, I hoped you would forgive me for something that happened . . . "

So, that's why she bought me this dress! I suddenly was glad for what happened to it.

Buzzard's delicate, clever composition was the result of his hard work and my determined efforts to keep him interested in class. Buzzard turned out to be both smart and sane. He was simply bored out of his very bright head.

During my early years as a teacher, I approached a student like Buzzard as a drill sergeant in the Marines might approach a sarcastic, slovenly private. I tried to break his spirit through a series of punishments and humiliations. Unfortunately, in an environment where one cannot spontaneously demand a thousand pushups or a six-mile run through the jungle, such a tactic is of limited effectiveness. After years of struggle with students like Buzzard, I changed from trying to quell their spirit to helping them learn to redirect it.

So, instead of punishing Buzzard for writing stories filled with gore, I let him have his blood and guts, but tried to direct his efforts toward a constructive end—his budding talent as a writer. Still, I refused to put up with any nonsense. If Buzzard interrupted me with the sound of yet another 747 crashing, I still sent him out of the room. But, philosophically, I had much more success working with him than against him. When I stopped trying to control his every thought and deed, I accepted Buzzard for who he was—a wild, creative, intelligent, belligerent, independent, angry thirteen-year-old with unfathomable gifts. Beats the heck out of a listless drone, at least in my book.

REFERENCES

Books

Block, Lawrence (1985). *Writing the Novel.* Cincinatti, OH: F&W Publications.
Britton, J., Burgess, T., Martin, N., McLeod, A., and Rosen, H. (1975). *The Development of Writing Abilities.* London: Macmillan, 11–18.
Campbell, Joseph, with Moyers, Bill, and Flowers, Betty, eds. (1988). *The Power of Myth.* New York: Doubleday & Company.
Crane, S. (1955). *Stories and Tales.* New York: Vintage Books.
Curtis, Christopher (1995). *The Watsons Go to Birmingham 1963.* New York: Bantam.
Gardner, John (1985). *The Art of Fiction.* New York: Vintage.
Kinneavy, J. (1971). *A Theory of Discourse.* New York: W. W. Norton.
Kirby, Liner, and Vinz (1988). *Inside Out.* Portsmouth, NH: Heinemann.
Lamott, Anne (1995). *Bird by Bird.* New York: Alfred A. Knopf.
Lipsyte, R. (1967). *The Contender.* New York: Bantam.
Osbon, D., ed. (1991). *A Joseph Campbell Companion.* New York: HarperCollins.
Paulsen, Gary (1995). *Harris and Me.* New York: Bantam.
Lorie, P., and Mascetti, M. (1996). *The Quotable Spirit.* New York: Macmillan, 79.

Music

"Traumerei" by Robert Schumann and "Reverie" by Claude Debussy. Recorded by Van Cliburn (1975). *The World's Favorite Piano Music.* BMG Classics. 0902660973–4.

Film

Stand by Me (1986). Directed by Rob Reiner. Starring River Phoenix, Wil Wheaton, Corey Feldman, and Jerry O'Connell. Columbia/Tri-star.

Poetry

"Break, Break, Break" by Alfred, Lord Tennyson
Sonnet 60 by William Shakespeare

OUTCOMES

1. Students used childhood experiences as fodder for compositions.

2. I came to know students on a personal level.

3. Students pondered (and wrote about) destiny and chance.

4. Students wrote in a variety of modes for different purposes.

5. Students used music, art, and graphs as catalysts for writing.

6. I discovered the brilliance of a defiant student.

7. Students synthesized several pieces of their writing into a single lengthy, coherent work.

ACTIVITIES

1. Read excerpts about childhood from some novels and biographies.

2. Engage students in conversations about where they were born; get them to focus upon their childhood.

3. Students list their eight biggest fears as a child.

4. Students list their top ten thrills.

5. Students write about an event, incident, or object from two perspectives.

6. Play some music about childhood and show some posters and works of art about childhood. Ask students to relate works of music and art to their childhood.

7. Students engage in show and tell about an object of significance.

8. Show a few minutes from the beginning of the film *Stand by Me.* Read descriptions of neighborhoods from *The Contender* and "The Blue Hotel."

9. Students draw maps and write descriptions of their old neighborhoods.

10. Read Shakespeare's Sonnet 60 and Tennyson's "Break, Break, Break."

11. Students create pie charts representing the time they spent doing different activities as a child.

12. Students begin the big paper in which they might synthesize previous shorter assignments into a coherent whole (or write a new paper).

13. Students ponder their destinies.

14. Students complete the final elaboration, peer edit, then give the paper to the teacher to evaluate.

3

AP Aliens

An interdisciplinary unit involving poetry, persuasion, myths, heroes, language, government, peace, war, and apologies

TIME: Three to five weeks; cooperative groups of two to three

There's a difference between being able to define a term and truly understanding what it means. Most of my eleventh-grade AP Language and Composition students could tell me that a hyperbole was a deliberate and sometimes outrageous exaggeration used for effect. Few of them, however, were able to identify a hyperbole when encountered in a text. Definitions don't mean much to me. I wanted students to understand and appreciate how a writer manipulates language for specific purposes.

I was growing impatient. I had been allowing my AP students the luxury of using a figurative language handout during their practice AP essays. Even with the handout, when my students would correctly identify some rhetorical technique, they seemed to have no clue as to *why* the author was using it. Instead, more often than not, they would answer my request for in-depth analysis by repeating terms, offering a definition, and then generalizing that an author was likely using such techniques "for effect."

These were intelligent students, many of them gifted and creative, yet I was failing to impress on them that it meant very little to correctly identify a specific technique if they could not explain how or why an author chose to use it. I wanted students to consider how a writer's choices affected the content, style, and artistic merit of a literary work.

The Birth of an Idea

During a graduate course in instructional technology I came across a Web site that caught my interest. I am a devout *Star Trek* fan of old, and when I stumbled upon a site of imaginary planets (see Figure 3.1), I was delighted. The planets were colorful and unique, and my first impulse was to question how I could link space travel to the language arts. I found thumbnail pictures of the planets at this site: http://sln.fi.edu/planets/gallery.html.

I paused only a second before I realized that I had found a potential answer to my AP dilemma. As I looked at the variety of planets it occurred to me that it might be possible to address figurative language from a more creative perspective, and in the process, I might be able to sneak in some other objectives as well.

"AP Aliens" began formulating in my head that night in class, but as I allowed my imagination to run, the original idea I had planned began to expand. By the following week I had developed a massive project that I anticipated lasting two to three weeks—one that would cover figurative language, critical thinking, analytical reasoning, rhetoric, poetry, essays, myths, heroes, predicting outcomes, comparison and contrast, and persuasive writing. The plan was simple—the students, in groups, would be required to create alien civilizations, complete with information on their society's demographics, history, and culture. Using a color printer, I printed out full-size pictures of the imaginary planets. Handout 3.1 is a sample of the figurative language handout I created specifically for this project.

FIGURE 3.1   Pictures of Fictional Planets

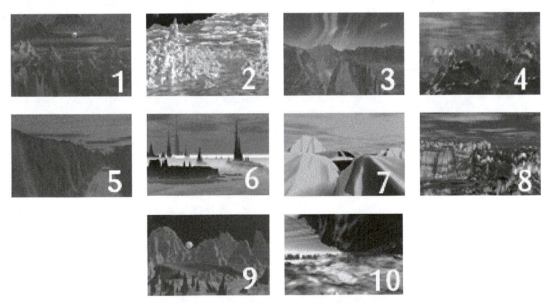

Images courtesy of the Franklin Institute Online, http://www.fi.edu/planets/gallery.html.

Figurative Language

Note: A more comprehensive list of terms and definitions can be found in most college handbooks, such as the Harbrace Handbook, *and at various Internet sites.*

1. **Alliteration**—also called head rhyme or initial rhyme, the repetition of the initial sounds (usually consonants) of stressed syllables in neighboring words or at short intervals within a line or passage, usually at word beginnings, as in "wild and woolly" or the line from Shelley's "The Cloud": "I bear light shade for the leaves when laid."
2. **Assonance**—the relatively close juxtaposition of the same or similar vowel sounds, but with different end consonants in a line or passage, thus a vowel rhyme, as in the words, *date* and *fade.*
3. **Consonance**—a pleasing combination of sounds; sounds in agreement with tone. Also, the repetition of the same end consonants of words such as *boat* and *night* within or at the end of a line, or the words, *cool* and *soul,* as used by Emily Dickinson in the third stanza of "He Fumbles at Your Spirit."
4. **Simile**—a figure of speech in which an explicit comparison is made between two essentially unlike things, usually using like, as, or than, as in Burns's, "O, my Luve is like a red, red rose" or Shelley's "As still as a brooding dove," in "The Cloud."
5. **Metaphor**—a comparison without the use of like or as, usually a comparison between something that is real or concrete and something that is abstract, e.g., Life is a dream.
6. **Personification**—a kind of metaphor that gives inanimate objects or abstract ideas human characteristics (The wind sang softly in the dark).
7. **Onomatopoeia**—the use of words in which the sounds seem to resemble the sounds they describe (hiss, buzz, bang).
8. **Hyperbole**—a deliberate, often outrageous exaggeration that is used for serious or comic effect (I'm so hungry I could eat a horse).
9. **Understatement**—the opposite of hyperbole. It is a kind of irony that deliberately represents something as much less than it really is (I could survive on two million dollars a year).
10. **Paradox**—a statement that contradicts itself. It may seem almost absurd, but usually turns out to have a coherent meaning, and often reveals a truth that is normally hidden (The more you know, the more you don't know).
11. **Pun**—a play on words that are identical or similar in sound, but have sharply diverse meanings. (In *Romeo and Juliet,* the dying Mercutio says, "Ask for me tomorrow, and you shall find me a grave man.")
12. **Allusion**—a reference to a mythological, literary, historical, or biblical person, place, or thing. (He met his Waterloo.)

Sequence

Days 1 and 2: Students Select a Planet and Delve into Alien Concepts

I placed the pictures of the planets on a table in front of the classroom and asked the groups to come up, one at a time, and select the planet that the group found to be the most inspiring. Once all groups had selected a planet, I asked them to define an alien concept. There were a few puzzled looks, but hands went up quickly. One of my more analytical students ventured that an alien concept was "a concept that we are not capable of thinking of." Not bad. Several others felt that anything "alien" was something that we simply were not familiar with. The general response was rather animated, and the ensuing discussion provided an avenue for the kind of analytical thinking I had wanted.

The students were instructed that, as groups, they were to discuss their selected picture and invent a distinctive, indigenous alien race and culture. I asked students to "think in alien concepts" and gave them a general guideline of my expectations for the project. I provided them with the Handout 3.2, which outlined the specifics of what I wanted to see in writing, as well as some of the limitations that would become important in the days to follow.

The groups began to buzz. I walked around, listening to the excited banter. I marveled at the imaginative twists students were already discussing. On occasion I would hear one student pointing out, "That's too human," or another arguing over some specific detail of the new race. I had intended for this phase to last only

---

HANDOUT **3.2**

Alien Concepts—A Guideline

Provide a complete physical description of your invented species, paying close attention to all details of appearance. Also with this description should be any personality traits that distinguish them from humans.

Next, create a history for your planet and a culture for your invented species. Think long-term for this and include such aspects as cities, towns, dwelling places, economy, government/rulership, family structure (if any), etc. Once again, think in terms of alien concepts—reach for ideas beyond human comprehension. Please be as thorough as possible, leaving out nothing that would tell about your race. One note: Your race does have the technology for space travel, as well as limited military strength, but cannot destroy planets or wipe out civilizations. How they travel and what type of weapons they have is up to you; just know your capabilities.

Next, create a system of beliefs for your race and its culture. Please base these beliefs on completely alien concepts, leaning more toward mythology than any current or past beliefs or religions known to humans. With an explanation of this system, please describe any modes of worship that may take place.

one day, but it became obvious that the class was engaged, and to allow them the time they needed to produce something of quality, I extended the first phase an extra day.

Kristen, Jennifer, and Zeke's group developed an alien race from the planet Borontnia (see Figure 3.2) that they were very proud of. In response to the handout, they wrote the following description.

Borontnia: Land of the Feeblejeebs

Family Structure—None. Marriage and parenting does not exist.

Religion—Though not worshipped, some Feeblejeebs of Borontnia's past are admired and remembered by statues in the Tantarf compound. The only time all four social classes gather is the snarfaly-celebrated festival honoring Valderax.

Economy—The Feeblejeebs are self sufficient and depend on each other to live. When you work, you are given everything you need.

Society—The Feeblejeebs live in harmony among their age classes. The Feeblejeeb developmental stage inside a "parent" Feeblejeeb is one snarfel. After birth, it takes a Feeblejeeb about one snarfel (snarfel = eighteen revolutions of the moon around Borontnia) to be fully grown. The Feeblejeeb society is an agist society where the aliens are ranked by their ages. The city of Valdraxia, the only inhabitation on Borontnia, was based on the agist concept. The city is circular with dwelling places for the separate classes around the circumference. From birth to four snarfels, a Feeblejeeb is a Prufnia. Working on the outer level of the city, the Prufnias are in charge of building materials. They take the cabata shells and process them into proper material for the building of dwellings. It is the Prufnia stage when Feeblejeebs receive their psychokinetic ability. The next level is the working place of Sicnifftas, who are five to seven snarfels old. Sicnifftas harvest the cabatas for the feeding of the city. The next class, from eight to eleven snarfels, is the Neebtar stage. The Neebtars deal with technology and defense. The standing army in Borontnia is the Neebtarian Regime. In the inner circle lives the Tantarfs. The Tantarfs are the respected elders over 12 snarfels. They have served their time as workers and now spend their time ruling over the city and relaxing. The monarch over Borontnia, a Sphencistraw, is always a Tantarf. All Tantarfs are considered to be of royalty. The monarch, the Sphencistraw, makes decisions with his nine council members for the good of his people.

Physical Description—A full-grown Feeblejeeb has a small, cylindrical body. Its insides are held together by stretchy bone-like structures. Two appendages exist on their lower bodies as a main source of transportation, and long toes create better balance in rough terrain. Two lightweight fins protrude from their backs for ooblek swimming. The Feeblejeebs have a long scar-like area on their side for the birth of new Feeblejeebs. Since the Feeblejeebs are genderless, each feeblejeeb carries a gene to reproduce at the age of seven snarfels. The pointed, oblong head of the species sits horizontally on the top of the body. Light sensors engulf the head to receive sight-like abilities. Two antennai distend from the head to send and receive psychokinetic messages from other Feeblejeebs. The pale gray outside covering of the body is scales in constant need of ooblek moisture.

FIGURE 3.2   The Planet Borontnia

Image courtesy of the Franklin Institute Online, http://www.fi.edu/planets/gallery.html.

Day 3: Myths of Origin

The next phase was to introduce the students to a few myths of origin and the concept of the archetypal hero and his journey. For the myths I located several Web sites that provided some brief origin myths that concisely illustrated the concept. I liked the myths at this Web site because they concisely illustrated the concept behind an origin myth and provided students with a model, or format, of what was to be expected of them. The first creation myth I used was "The Battle between the Gods and Titans"—the origin of Zeus and the Greek Gods, as well as the origin of lightning. The second myth I used was "The Story of Arachne and Athena"—Arachne being the first spider. After we had read the short myths, I led the class in a discussion of other tales of origins that they might have been told. Many students recited tales told to them by grandparents, parents, uncles, and aunts.

To address the hero, I found a Web site dedicated to Joseph Campbell, author of *The Hero with a Thousand Faces,* that was set up with short explanations and clear distinctions of the "recognizable hero who appears again and again throughout world mythology." Campbell's archetypal hero typically goes on a quest, which takes him through three different levels—the departure (separation), the journey (initiation), and the return. It is after the return that the hero completes his quest, usually by bringing new ideas, concepts, or ways of living back home.

I found bits and pieces on the Web site that were perfect for discussing Campbell's conception of the hero. Many students brought up current celebrities, mostly singers and movie stars. Some of them mentioned historical figures such as Christopher Columbus, George Washington, or Leif Erickson. During the discussion, Kurt Cobain (deceased lead singer of the rock band Nirvana) was a popular choice, and I was pleased to witness students struggling to place him in the critical "return" phase of his journey. I heard one girl argue that Kurt Cobain had given up during his "initiation" phase and could not be considered a hero. Several other students disagreed with her and sought to rationalize their perceptions of Cobain as hero.

A few members of the class mapped out the journey of such mythological figures as Perseus and Hercules. I was satisfied. I witnessed the engagement and thought process I was hoping for, and was ready to lay out the next phase in their AP alien project.

Day 4: Heroes and Myths

Having given the students some background on myths of origin and archetypal heroes, each group was instructed to create a myth of origin for their invented species as well as a legendary hero. I instructed the class that the myth and the hero were not to be connected directly. To ease any confusion and to provide the groups with some written directives, I created Handout 3.3.

HANDOUT **3.3**

On Origins and Heroes

Myth of Origin
Using the provided myths of origin as a model, your group is to create a myth of origin for your invented alien race. Please incorporate the alien concepts of your species into a myth that explains the origin of one or more aspects of your invented society. This myth should be written as a very short story (not an explanation of what it would be about).

Legendary Hero
Using the stages of Campbell's archetypal hero, all groups should create a legendary hero for their invented culture. Please combine Campbell's stages with the uniqueness of your alien hero to create a short story telling of the deeds (or whatever) of your hero, and what it is they did that made them a hero (please write this in a story format, and not an explanation). Provided with the hero stories, all groups must provide an analysis describing the similarities and differences between the qualities and characteristics of their invented species hero and those of a human hero. Also, each group must create a short poem (or ode) honoring your hero, and telling your hero's story. In these poems please include the following figurative language: *alliteration, assonance, simile,* and *personification*. Finally, each group must provide a color illustration of their hero (effort counts here, not artistic talent).

Following are three student samples of what Kristen's group did in response to the handout: the Feeblejeeb myth of origin, their hero story, and their hero poem.

Myth
by Kristen's Group

Long ago before the birth of the many, the planet of Borontnia was a vastly different place. On its surface dwelt two different races, the Feeblejeebs and the Smeargouls. The Smeargouls were similar to the Feeblejeebs, having evolved from the same ancestor, but had a few distinguising characteristics. They had much greater physical strength than the Feeblejeebs but lacked any psyonic abilities. The Feeblejeebs and Smeargouls lived in small communities scattered around the planet, geographically and culturally isolated.

After many eons of peaceful existence, a time of much hardship occurred. Solar radiation from the nearby star had dried up most of the oobleck, and kabatas were scarce to be found. Instead of sharing in the existing supplies, a group of Smeargouls viscously attacked a Feeblejeeb settlement and pillaged all the kabatas. This action startled many of both races, but as time passed and conditions worsened, the Smeargouls began repeating their attacks. In response to the massive threat to their race's survival, the Feeblejeebs banded together into large armed communities. The Smeargouls similarly came together to combat the Feeblejeebs. Even after conditions returned to normal on the planet, the two races were now in conflict. As years passed the wars became more violent.

Living in a time of war, many ways to kill large numbers of the opposing race were developed and copied. As neither side gained any significant advantage, the technological development increased. Than a brilliant Feeblejeeb, named Enceladious, developed a weapon called the bioeradicator. With this weapon, huge areas could be eradicated with a moment's notice. When the Feeblejeebs flaunted this to their opponent, the Smeargouls quickly developed their own. The Feeblejeebs and Smeargouls continued to build newer and better bioeradicators to counter their opponents, and kept trying to find ways to respond quickly to any use.

As tensions mounted, some Smeargouls raided a small Feeblejeeb city and looted it. Convinced of a larger attack, the Feeblejeebs aimed their bioeradicator at the Smeargoul cities and fired. The Smeargouls fired back before they were destroyed. As the energy fields cleared, little was left of either race, and great black scars in the landscape stretched as far as the mind could detect. The great peoples had been shattered, and little life remained anywhere on Borontnia. The small remnants that were left had to struggle to survive in the ruins of the land.

So began the age of Thanate, when small nomadic tribes desperately searched for food in the ruins of the once great civilizations. Little is known of the times of old, save that in the end, their own genius and marvels doomed them. Learn well from the mistakes of the past, otherwise they will be repeated in the future. True power rests not in the ability to destroy, but the ability to create.

With the completion of the myth, I questioned the group as to what exactly was being created—what origin was being presented? Kristen, the group leader, argued that it was the tale of how nomadic tribes came to be on Borontnia, and how the landscape came to be as rugged as it was. I was curious as to whether this was a myth or a history, and was told that this was simply a tale that had been passed on through the ages.

Borontnia's Hero: Valderax
Group 5's Hero Story

Many, many snarfels ago, the Feeblejeebs of Borontnia wandered the planet in a nomadic search for food. Scarce food was to be found on the dry, desolate planet. The war between the Smeargouls and the Feeblejeebs had diminished, and though the enemy had retreated, the land was left in ruins. The Feeblejeebs were forced to become vagabonds and roam the land in herds. They had no hope; nothing in their future. As Feeblejeebs began to lose their will to live, many, especially Tantarfs, laid their massive bodies on the cold land and waited to die.

One Neebtarian Feeblejeeb named Valderax wandered the planet with a group of migrants in the time after the war. A Tantarf that traveled with the group, Fumphelgok, saw something in Valderax that no one else saw. One cold night, Fumphelgok told Valderax of its visions of glory and honor for Valderax. Fumphelgok knew that Valderax was Borontnia's only hope. So, Valderax, on the insistence of Fumphelgok, left the group in search of hope for its fellow Feeblejeebs. Alone, and not knowing what it was looking for, Valderax walked for a snarfel. It encountered mountains that touched the moon, ooblek rivers too wide to cross, and cold nights that froze its scaly skin. On one occasion, Valderax came across Stixreem, an evil Smeargoul general left from the war. After a fight that lived into the night, Valderax killed Stixreem and continued on his journey to find some oddly shaped rocks. What he had found was a land abundant with cabata, a food Feeblejeebs consumed that was found in jagged rock casings. The land was flat and supplied with ooblek lakes. Valderax knew the suffering Feeblejeebs could use the land. Valderax ran back and found his nomadic group, along with many others, to tell them of this land of plenty. Within two snarfels, the empire of Valdraxia had been built and the Feeblejeebs never went hungry again.

Although not the strongest of hero legends, Valderax fits the criteria of the archetypal hero. It was interesting to watch as my students created parallels between the common human hero and that of their alien heroes. Repeatedly, the heroes of the different alien races would confront evil, and always they would return home. Not only were the students becoming increasingly engaged in their ongoing project, they were also beginning to develop a concept of the hero as well as an appreciation for the role of the hero in contemporary society.

Valderax
Poem by Kristen's Group

In times long gone in lands of old,
Beneath the sky so dark and cold,
Dwelt the remnants of the Feeblejeebs,
Long diminished by years of war.

In scattered tribes like hungry wolves,
In the shattered remains of a once great world,
Was born one by the name of Valderax,
The bringer of a new age.

Valderax was a giant among his kind,
With courage and honor and an incredible mind,
As strong as a Smeargoul and as swift as a chake,
He strove a better future for his people to make.

He left his tribe on the lonely stones,
The cold night wrapped its blanket round his bones,
As he set out to meet his fate,
Bathed in the silvery light of Faerate.

As he leapt and crept and walked many a step,
He chanced upon a bubbling brook,
Then he heard a strange noise and decided to look,
And out from behind a bush a cruel Smeargoul swept.

Valderax battled his foe and the very earth shook,
And at last the Smeargoul lay dead in the bubbly brook,
And Valderax resumed his arduous task,
To find a home where his people could last.

After many a journey and the passage of time,
A land was found, peaceful and sublime,
And back to his people a trip Valderax took,
To bring them all to live and to look.

And so ended the long age of the name Thanate,
And all Feeblejeebs rose up in great glee,
For a home had been found and now they could live,
Forevermore in peace and prosperity.

While the poem is simple, figurative language abounds. Given the difficult time constraints (one class period for the group to complete all aspects of the myth and hero), Kristen's group did a decent job. Note the personification in the fourth stanza, second line: "The cold night wrapped its blanket round his bones" (good use, but the hero has now taken on a gender in a genderless society). Alliteration is

FIGURE 3.3   The Hero Valderax

present—"bubbling brook . . . peace and prosperity"—though not terribly dynamic. Similes and assonance are abundant throughout the poem. In assessing this particular piece, time constraints were given consideration and the work deemed adequate for an average score in the low to mid B range.

Days 5 and 6: Presentations of Alien Cultures

Day 5 was oral presentation day. I explained to the groups that at this point they would be explaining their invented race to the classroom. The students were not aware of my plans to catapult their aliens into a sudden war, so I simply told them that if they wished to do well on the remainder of this project, it would be imperative that each individual take intensely copious notes on the invented species that their fellow classmates would be introducing. I allowed each group up to fifteen minutes for their presentation and requested that they explain their alien species in detail, read their myth of origins, introduce and read their hero stories and poems, and discuss the differences that set their hero apart from the human arche-type. I was surprised that fifteen minutes proved insufficient for most groups, and that the students listening to the presentations responded with so many high-level questions. I was also impressed with the amount of genuine respect and interest shown toward each group's creativity and at the obvious pride that the groups had shown while discussing their invented alien cultures.

Days 7 and 8: The Epic Alien War

When all the presentations were done and all the notes taken, I began what would become known to my students (and many students who weren't in my class) as the "epic alien war." I set it up so that each planet had one planet to attack (in a round robin sort of fashion). No planet was being attacked by the same planet that they were attacking. Based on the notes taken during the presentations, it was each group's job to devise as clever a strategy as possible to destroy the alien race that they were assigned to attack. With this attack came a variety of writing require-ments as well as the need for a subjective reason as to why they were the aggres-sors in this impending battle. To clarify my expectations to the class, I provided the information in Handout 3.4.

With the onset of the war plans, the class environment became interestingly dif-ferent. There was a serious intensity in the groups that I hadn't anticipated. It occurred to me that they were worried for the safety of their invented race. Kristen's group talked in low tones, and as I sat in for a moment on their "war conference" I was stunned to hear Zeke persuade them toward a plan for total genocide. Zeke was

---

HANDOUT 3.4

The War

Each group must decide on their reasons for attacking their assigned planet, and based on their notes about this culture, devise a plan of attack for maximum destruction (for example, if attacking a planet of giant slugs, salt bombs would be an intimidating weapon). This plan should be written out, detailing and sequencing each stage of the intended attack, and giving reasons why this strategy will work. Also include anticipated retaliation, defenses, and possible problems that may arise during this battle. With this battle strategy, all groups must provide a scenario of intended outcomes, costs, timelines, and forecasted casualties. Finally, each group will need to write a formal letter to the planet they are attacking. This letter must explain their reasons for declaring war, must explain their intentions, and must sound sincere and convincing. To help create a better letter, the following figurative language should be included: *hyperboles, onomatopoeia, a rhetorical question(s),* and *parallel structure.* Once again, groups should think in terms of alien concepts and base all war decisions on these concepts. Note: it may be helpful for groups to keep their target planets and battle plans a well-guarded secret.

reviving the bioeradicator from the war with the Smeargouls and was leading Kristen and Jennifer into a finely detailed, precision attack that would annihilate the Snordsfs, leaving the planet of Shredlof a desolate and barren rock. While Zeke began feeding the details to Kristen, Jennifer composed the following war declaration.

Declaration of War

To all who inhabit Shredlof:

Over many snarfels, the Tantarfs of Borontnia have observed your culture. It appears that your physical features parallel the features of our worst adversary, the Smeargouls! Your presence in the universe is a constant reminder of our struggle, our strife, and our loss. Is this not reason enough to annihilate your civilization? As you receive this declaration, the Neebtarian Regime is coming to destroy your planet. We hope you hear the whizz of aircraft, the booms of our guns, and the sizzle of our powerful bioeradicators that echo to the ends of the universe. Your existence disgusts the Feeblejeebs of Borontnia, and we make no apologies. In your last moment of existence, remember that the Feeblejeebs will prevail with unending force over all who are related to the Smeargouls.

Day 9: Learning the Fine Arts of Negotiation and Persuasion

After all war plans had been composed and revised, the groups were asked one at a time to stand up and read their declarations of war. Once again, only this time without encouragement, the groups were to take notes and ask questions. At times, the environment became heated, as groups under attack offered emotional rebuttals explicating why those attacking them would fail. When it came time for Kristen's group to read their declaration of war, Zeke was the first one to the front of the room. Zeke read his group's declaration eloquently and arrogantly, pausing to make sure that the creators of the Snordsf were taking him seriously. When he was done, Kristen and Jennifer elaborated on the attack plan, explaining how *their* bioeradicator had been enhanced, and on how thoroughly and completely they were going to destroy all carbon-based life on Shredlof.

Lara, leader of group 3, the creators of the Snordsf race, smiled widely at the conclusion of Kristen's war declaration. Many of the students from other groups began snickering and talking amongst themselves. With only a moment's pause, Lara held up her hand and informed Kristen's group that they had clearly stated during their original alien presentation that the Snordsfs were *not* a carbon-based life form. Kristen and Jennifer looked accusingly at Zeke. Zeke colored a bit and then matter-of-factly informed Lara that they would land and fight hand-to-hand if need be. I ended the period informing them that I would have to evaluate the attacks, and that I would have more information for the next class as to the status of their invented race. Many of the students left the class that day in very animated discussions.

Days 10 and 11: Peace and Alliances

The class was anxious to find out the fates I had decided for their aliens, and quieted quickly for me. I informed them that, due to the unanticipated attack from a second planet, all of the alien cultures had suffered massive casualties, and had expended most of their weapons. I went on to explain that they were now anticipating a retaliation from the planet that they had attacked, and that with such retaliation, they would surely face annihilation.

There were moans, some nods, a few smiles, and a few worried looks. I informed the groups that it would now be necessary for each group to prepare two peace proposals—one to the planet they attacked, and one to the planet that had attacked them. I apprised the students that, at this point, if any group declined to accept their peace offering, their invented culture would most likely be annihilated. I informed them that on the off chance they didn't accept the peace that was offered them, but everyone else accepted their peace offering, they could prevail. The letters would become the deciding factor as to whether their invented aliens would live or die. Built into these letters were several AP objectives, including some serious persuasive writing and some detailed comparing and contrasting. To give the students a clear understanding of what I expected, once again, I provided a handout (see Handout 3.5).

It was apparent immediately that many of the groups were reluctant to write a peace proposal to a planet they had, for the most part, insulted on the previous day. I emphasized the need for them to write sincere letters that would be accepted, and reminded them that if the letters were not accepted, they very well could end the lives of their invented aliens. The groups understood what I was saying, and, once again, I was impressed with the creativity they showed in their persuasiveness, while still satisfying the criteria for use of figurative language.

HANDOUT **3.5**

Peace

Due to the unanticipated attack from a second planet, your planet has suffered massive casualties and expended most of its weapons and resources. You are now anticipating retaliation from the planet you initially attacked, and with such retaliation, you face annihilation. Each group must prepare two peace proposals—one to the planet you have attacked and one to the planet that has attacked you. Each letter must be distinctly different in that you were the aggressors of one attack and the recipients of another. Each letter must be very persuasive as to why peace between the planets is possible and must also highlight a strong comparison and contrast of their cultures and civilizations. To help facilitate the success of these letters the following figurative language should be included: *synecdoche, parallel structure,* and *understatement.* Lastly, as a gesture of sincerity, each group should create a poem to go with each letter, honoring their foe's legendary hero. In these poems, include *consonance, assonance,* and an *allusion* to their own hero.

While Kristen's group had attempted to annihilate the Snordsfs in their initial attack, the Sibilotaxians, the group who had been assigned to attack Kristen's group, had devised a rather brutal assault on the Feeblejeebs. First they had taken the Tantarf Council as prisoners; then they had demanded instant surrender for relocation for their home planet, Xantrolobis. They did offer a "willingness" to allow the Feeblejeebs to exist as slaves. Now they were in the precarious position of attempting peace with what had turned out to be the most ruthless of alien races. The following is the peace proposal that was submitted *to* Kristen's group.

Dear Feeblejeebs of Borontnia,

On behalf of all Sibilotaxians, the Zooglick Counsel would like to apologize for our previous aggressions toward your civilization. Our actions were hasty and we were not fully informed about your ways when we attacked. We now realize that our societies are much too different to coexist on one planet despite our common activity in the dark. Your people would achieve no great benefit from our great Zoogla, so we withdraw all previous demands for your relocation and hope you will forgive our supreme arrogance. As a token of our goodwill, we return your Tantarf Council unharmed. They were treated with the utmost respect while on Xantrolobis; they are wise elders and, we are sure, will lead the Feeblejeebs to follow peaceful paths from now on. We wish to ally ourselves with your great might, but we request that you destroy the bioeradicators, which present a small barrier to true trust and peace. We ask not for ourselves, but for the less able in the universe incapable of defending themselves. Our Wohkannae were quick to act, and always will be when a great danger approaches, but we no longer feel any reason your planet and ours should not be on good terms with each other. We wish to perpetuate all life throughout the galaxy, please recall we never threatened your people with extinction, and help those less fortunate creatures around us. Please seriously consider accepting our friendship and support to form what could be the strongest alliance in our historical memories. Again, we apologize and beg your forgiveness for our unprovoked attack on your mighty city Valdraxia; we only thought we were doing the cautious thing and we honestly and earnestly wished good things for you on Xantrolobis. We anxiously await your reply.

Humbly Yours,
The Zooglick Counsel

The offer in this letter to form an alliance is interesting because it ultimately saved the Sibilotaxians from total annihilation at the conclusion of this project. The letter is solid in its objective, to obtain peace, and it does contain the requested figurative language. The "bioeradictors, which present a small barrier to true trust and peace," is the understatement, and the reference to "our great Zoogla" is representative of the whole Sibilotaxian race, therefore a decent synecdoche. The comparison and contrast is weak, simply stating that their "societies are much too different ... despite our common activity...", but the parallel structure reoccurs nicely throughout the entire letter, "They were treated ... they are wise ... we wish ... we request ... we ask. . . ." Once again, realizing the time constraints of this assignment for assessment purposes, the work is considered decent, the figurative language use and persuasive writing is slightly above average, and aside from the weak comparison and contrast, the effort exhibited was good—a score in the range of a B+ was merited.

Days 12 and 13: Peer Editing Proposals for Peace

At this point my AP classes had become absorbed in alien cultures. I had never before witnessed such complete immersion from students in a cooperative setting. Not only were the students striving to fulfill the criteria set forth in the activities, they were doing so competitively and pushing each other to be more creative in the process. With the passing of the letters at this point, all groups would be accepting or declining peace, and in the process, deciding whether their invented aliens would live or die. If all accepted peace, then all would live. If all except one accepted peace, then the one who chose to attack would annihilate the peace-seeking planets. If more than one group declined peace, then it would be up to me as judge to decide who survived and who faced annihilation.

I instructed all groups to pass the letters and poems to the prospective planets with which they sought peace. What I required was that each group come prepared with a variety of colored highlighters and that they begin analyzing the letters and poems for the figurative language specified. Also, I required that each group analyze the letters for sincerity. Handout 3.6 explains specifically what I expected and points out the importance of accepting or declining peace.

Figure 3.4 is an example of the analyzed (and color-coded) letter that Kristen's group wrote to the Sibilotaxians; Figure 3.5 is the poem honoring the Sibilotaxian hero, Largoid.

HANDOUT **3.6**

The Letters

Each group must analyze letters for sincerity as well as figurative language. Groups should divide the letters received as well as the poems so that all members share equally in the work. Using the criteria from the "Peace" handouts, all groups should underline, color-code, or label (or whatever works) the letters and poems, showing very clearly where the figurative language occurs and its relative effectiveness. *No group may talk to another group during the analysis.* When the figurative language has been found and identified, each group must then write a letter answering the letters analyzed. Peace must be accepted or declined in these letters. Please discuss your reasons for accepting or declining peace in your letter (be as persuasive as possible), and also reveal your analysis of their figurative language. Be sure to assess the effectiveness and correctness of the language used. While explaining their use of figurative language, *use examples from their poems and letters to make your point.* Please be cautious in writing these letters and make sure you have satisfied all requirements in this phase of the assignment—my assessment of these letters will determine the outcome of the war and the prospects for peace.

FIGURE 3.4 Letter to Sibilotaxians

Sibilotaxians

Most honorable Sibilotaxians,
We humbly regret any actions of ours
which may have offended you or your
Morals. In our rash actions, we may have
annihilated an innocent [innocent] peoples who have never
lifted a hand against us. Recognizing the
error of our ways and the destruction
we may have purpetrated. With this reliocation
we gladly propose the following concessions as
per your recommendations in your declaration of
war. The following will be done with the
upmost speed and percission; precision

- All bioeradicators will be immediately destroyed,
  dissassembled, and forgotten as per your
  askence.
- The city of Valdraxia will be immediately surrendered
  on the following conditions-
  1. No further violence will occur once all
     hands have laid down their weapons.
  2. Our Tantarts will be returned unharmed
  3. Immediate negotiations of peace and friendship
     will occur between our races un the surrender of
     the city.
- Our people will remain on Valdraxia while
  your proposal said that you wished to bring
  the light to us, you truely have in many
  ways. Your knowledge of peacefull and succesful
  lifestyles will greatly influence our future actions.
  Yet Barotnia is our home, and I fear
  that we would fare poorly in a world like
  yours since we have evolved into greatly different
life styles.
- The valdraxian troops will immediately
disengaged dissengauge from the sredlofian
system and immediatly make amends for
our genocidal actions.

I hope if we can agree on such a proposal of
peace and friendship our races can develop a
constructive relationship through wich our peoples
will learn from eachother. I hope any small
misunderstandings we have had can be quickly corrected.

Sincerely,
Zanthir, Sphen x istraw of
Valdraxia

FIGURE 3.5   Poem Honoring Largoid

Where the light of the pure has never reached,
In the dark of space so far and deep,
Was the moon of the dead that shed no light,
A friend to all those who lurked in the night.

This dark fearful moon was quite cruelly inclined,
And decided to spark fear in each Sctartartans mind,
[Sibolertowan]
For it maad and it moaned and it muted the sun,
And it made life for the Estroldians not very fun

In this shadow cast by the shape of the Largon,
The people suffered and whithered in dark,
They tried and they tried to get rid of this threat,
Yet each attempt was not with success met.

[Amongst]
Kanoxt was a Vardagoid, a hardworking sort,
Who saved his race from this spectre of wort,
Like another we know he set out at night,
To for his people a great battle fight

He Spun and he swam as if out of a gun,
And to the rogue largoid he had finally come,
He burrowed inside with all his great might,
And showed the dark moon the truth of the light.

The results of the analysis gave credence to the assignment. Where the Feeblejeebs appeared hasty, and the writing showed an abundance of spelling and syntactic errors, the Sibilotaxians were diligent in highlighting the errors. In their written analysis and letter accepting peace, the Sibilotaxian "Zoogla Counsel" was equally as thorough, using direct examples as I had requested.

To the Feeblejeebs:

We have read and thoroughly analyzed your terms for peace between our races, as outlined in your letter. After much consideration, we have decided to accept your peace.

We have also carefully and tediously analyzed your use of figurative language in your letter, and though we found your spelling outrageously horrendous, most other aspects proved satisfactory.

We immediately identified your synecdoche. The phrase ". . . while your proposal said that you wished to bring the light to us . . . " clearly indicated that the "light" represented our knowledge and understanding. Your use of parallel structure was very obvious as well to us: "will be immediately surrendered . . . will occur once all hands . . . friendship and peace will occur, our people will remain . . . " all indicated your knowledge and understanding. Your understatement, as well, proved to be sufficient.

However, we do regret that we have found several flaws. We feel quite compelled to inform you that "Recognizing the error of our ways and the destruction we may have perpetuated" is not a complete sentence, and has no effect as a fragment.

We felt honored by your poem and admire your use of consonance, rhyme, alliteration, and assonance.

We are very optimistic and enthusiastic about our union and expect great things to come as a result. We are elated that you have willingly destroyed your bioeradicators and all knowledge of them.

We respect your decision to remain in your fair city of Valdraxia. As requested, we will deliver your Tantarfs safely along with this letter. We feel strongly that any more conflict would be quite unnecessary, and possibly harmful to both of our races. We are greatly pleased to be able to accept your terms and wish you the best in future Zoogs.

Your Humble Allies,
The Zoogla Council

Day 14: Writing a Cause and Effect Wrap-up Paper

For the final phase of this project it was necessary for me to make a decision. Ideally, all groups would have sought and accepted peace, and the next and final phase of the project would move forward smoothly. In the case of this particular class, group 1 (the "Brobs of Nijeskatie") had decided not to accept peace, citing that "the context of your letter leads us to believe that, although a temporary peace could be attained, a long-lasting peace may not be possible."

While, technically, this nonacceptance should have annihilated the Sibilotaxians, I found myself rather intrigued by the alliance that the Zooglick Council had formed with the Feeblejeebs. If I understood the alliance correctly, the Brobs would now have to defeat both the Sibilotaxians *and* the Feeblejeebs.

I was pretty sure of what was right here, but in order to assuage any doubts, I stopped Kristen before class began and informed her that the Sibilotaxians had been attacked, and asked her if the Feeblejeebs would honor their alliance. Kristen was concerned for her group's Feeblejeebs, and asked me what the outcome would be if they did honor the alliance. I told her that I would have to decide that based on a new battle strategy, and that there was the possibility of the Feeblejeebs being annihilated. I was bluffing, but I wanted a concrete solution to the fate of the Brobs and the Sibilotaxians. If Kristen honored the alliance, the Brobs would be annihilated. If not, the Sibilotaxians would vanish. Kristen paused only a moment and then, making what I considered to be an impressive decision, told me that the Feeblejeebs would honor their alliance.

The class was anxious. Most of them knew that the Brobs had not accepted peace. The Sibilotaxians were nervous. I informed the class that the Brobs had decided to attack the Sibilotaxians, and that under normal circumstances, they would have been victorious. Group 1, the Brobs, looked at me suspiciously.

"What do you mean, 'normal?'" asked Katie, the group leader of the Brobs.

"As it turned out," I answered, "through the peace process, the Sibilotaxians formed an alliance with the Feeblejeebs. When you attacked the Sibilotaxians, you also went to war with the Feeblejeebs. You never stood a chance, and your race has been annihilated."

The class was stunned. Three weeks into the project had yielded a surprisingly dramatic conclusion. The students in group 1 shook their heads in disbelief.

I still had a final assignment for the class. I informed the groups that as a wrap-up they had one last job to fulfill. I explained that their group had been contacted to create a proposal for an intergalactic planetary committee for future arbitration and dispute of any planet disagreements. I wanted the paper to be a cause-and-effect eye-opener, and I wanted the whole paper structured as a syllogism. Incorporated in the papers, I wanted to see at least three uses of rhetorical or figurative language. I requested that they highlight their techniques and catalogue them for easy identification.

No Slackers

To this day, many of my former students still enjoy talking of their alien races. One of my primary concerns with such an extensive project was assessment. To be honest, I placed very few grades on the written work. Early on, I made comments on their alien explanations, as well as on the myths and hero stories. I stated at the onset of the project that I would *not* be grading all of the writing done for this project, but that *all* of the writing done *was* subject to a grade. When I placed a grade on a specific part of the project, I used the handouts that were given as a rubric. The first question I ask myself during assessment is always, *What did I want and expect?* Given the assumption that the students understood my expectations, it then becomes a matter of assessing how well they met those expectations. To help myself stay consistent, I often take an index card and list the specifics of what I want for an A paper (e.g., Demonstrates depth and effort in writing; Good grasp of mechanics; Strong and repetitive use of figurative language).

The activities in "AP Aliens" were designed to force the students into specific AP style analysis and practice, and as the student engagement increased and my objectives were being met, there was very little need to do any grading. I did sit in with groups, reading what they were writing and giving them feedback, but the results I wanted for assessment would come with the practical applications I intended when the project finished.

"AP Aliens" was run completely as an in-class assignment, often giving the students very little time for the amount of collaboration and writing that was truly needed. The students would often sneak in separate pieces of the assignments that they had divided and taken home with them. I pretended not to notice. I found it wonderfully ironic that the students were actually assigning themselves home-work, and pretending they hadn't. Furthermore, all members of each group seemed personally invested in the outcome of "AP Aliens." Neither I, nor any members of the groups, could identify a single slacker in the entire class.

With the conclusion of "AP Aliens" there came a distinctive improvement in the analytical skills of my AP class. Before, they had struggled even to identify various rhetorical techniques. After this project, they not only identified rhetorical techniques, they also became adept at critiquing a text's eloquence and effective-ness. In subsequent compositions and essays, most students seemed to write with a new sense of confidence. Not only had they become adept at impressing each other, they had learned to impress themselves.

Adaptability

"AP Aliens" was created specifically for an Advanced Placement English class, but with its success, I found no reason not to attempt a variation of the project with a few of my regular English classes. In one particular tenth-grade class, I used a vari-ety of dragon pictures found on the Internet and had the students (a large class of vocal, rambunctious, and energetic young men) create "dragon cultures." The con-cept of the project was similar, but the skills incorporated into the specific assign-ments were different. For example, instead of the elevated emphasis on figurative language, I required such things as fragments used for effect, or sentences that mandated commas and numerous adjectives. I did introduce several of the figura-tive language terms to the class, and the results were impressive, but not on as grand a scale as with the AP classes.

Within the general population of the public school (and many private school) classrooms, there is a high variance in skill levels. The products of this project reflected these levels, and often I had to remind groups repeatedly to share the work. In adapting the assignment I found it necessary to incorporate several peer revision sessions within the groups, and I leaned heavily on my group leaders to become tutors. Overall, the classes demonstrated a high level of engagement during the projects, and they responded well to the expectations and high level of creativity that was demanded of them.

OUTCOMES

1. Students learned to use figurative language effectively.
2. Students learned ways to manipulate the language for rhetorical ends.
3. Students experienced a simulation of war, peace, and negotiation.
4. Students wrote several different kinds of writing.
5. Students learned about myths of origin.
6. Students learned and applied what they learned about archetypal heroes.
7. Students gained expertise on the art of negotitation.
8. Students eagerly participated in an interdisciplinary unit in which they learned much about government, religion, and history.

ACTIVITIES

1. Place students in groups of three to five.
2. Go over figurative language (handout).
3. Find alien landscapes. Have students select the most interesting terrain.
4. Students write a description of the landscape.
5. Students describe in writing the appearance of their race of aliens according to the guidelines.
6. Students describe in writing the history, government, and other aspects of the culture of their invented race.
7. Introduce students to myths of origin.
8. Read "Battle between the Gods and the Titans."
9. Read "Story of Arachne and Athena."
10. Discuss origin myths with which students are familiar.
11. Introduce students to the work of Joseph Campbell, especially those aspects that pertain to the archetypal hero and the quest.
12. Discuss historical and contemporary figures in terms of the hero archetype.
13. Students create a myth of origin and a legendary hero.

14. Students present information in an oral presentation on the history, government, and culturally significant aspects of their invented races.

15. Alert students that they should take careful notes on the alien races created by other groups.

16. Explain the nature of war in regard to their alien cultures.

17. Students attack or do not attack, and explain their reasoning.

18. Students learn about the outcomes of war.

19. Students write persuasive proposals to foster peace.

20. Students accept or reject peace proposals.

21. Students analyze proposals for effective use of figurative language and sincerity.

22. Students write final persuasive proposal.

4

Screenplays

Promoting reading, writing, thinking, and performance through the moving image

TIME: Three to five weeks

> *We all know and admit that film art has a greater influence on the minds of the general public than any other art. The official guardians of culture note the fact with a certain amount of regret and uneasiness. But too few of us are sufficiently alive to the dangers that are an inevitable consequence of this fact. Nor do we realize clearly enough that we must be better connoisseurs of the film if we are not to be as much at the mercy of perhaps the greatest intellectual and spiritual influence of our age as to some blind and irresistible elemental force.*
>
> —Marcus 1971, p. 29

Once upon a time, Frank, a vocational education teacher who taught courses on the repair of heating and air conditioning units at my school, took me aside, shook his finger in my face, and sternly admonished me for the way that I approached the teaching of secondary English.

"Baines, quit teaching those kids as if they are all going to be making a living writing novels. Teach them how to write for survival. Creative writing is stupid and irrelevant. These kids need to know how to fill out job applications and give good directions."

"Directions?" I asked. "Like how to get to the Wal-Mart without getting lost?"

"No. I mean directions for helping put things together. Kind of like technical writing. Students should be learning practical writing, not all this airy, fairy writing that you do. No one makes a living as a novelist anymore."

I smiled. "You are right about that, Frank. Few persons other than authors of blockbusters—Michael Crichton, John Grisham, and J. K. Rowling—are able to eke out a living by writing novels. But mastery of language is my goal, not the creation of a class of wannabe novelists. If a student can write a moving short story, I feel pretty certain that he could handle concocting directions for replacing a condenser."

"Kids should practice writing how they're going to write in real life," Frank said, unconvinced.

"They will have all their lives to practice filling out forms and applications," I said. "But few of them will ever be asked again to put down on paper what is in their heads and their hearts."

"You really want them to put that on paper?" Frank asked. "If you're interested in getting at what kids really feel, you should turn your class into a studio. Most of these kids have been raised on MTV and haven't read a book since *Charlotte's Web*."

"Hey, you know that's an excellent idea, Frank," I said.

"What, you're gonna start teaching kids how to write for MTV?" Frank said with a snicker.

"No, but your ideas about turning the classroom into a studio and appealing to a student's sense of the visual are great. Thanks."

Shortly after my conversation with Frank, I began thinking how I could work screenwriting into the secondary language arts curriculum. Personally, I have always found viewing a film—moving into a dark room where other stimuli do not intervene and becoming engrossed in an expertly photographed, carefully orchestrated, and auditorially enhanced multimedia experience—to have a profound effect upon how I view the world.

As a gawky, freckle-faced adolescent who saw too many James Bond movies, I spent innumerable hours gazing in the mirror, working on how I might start attracting the attention of girls. From saying "hello" (use an English accent, smile with cool assurance, always act like everything is casual and under control) to more advanced "make-out techniques" (grab the girl, smash your lips fully against hers, and fall onto a couch; expect her to slug you at first, but eventually she'll become mesmerized by your kiss), I based my crude and crummy moves on Sean Connery's suave interpretation of 007.

Certainly, I'm not the only person who has ever been influenced by a movie. More than a century ago, when the Lumiere brothers showed a jumpy, primitive film of a train traveling down a track toward the camera, the Paris crowd vacated the screening room in a panic. Over the past twenty years, the American Educational Research Association, the American Psychological Association, and other organizations have issued policy statements acknowledging the power of film to influence human behavior. Film can convincingly present the unreal as real and the real as fiction. Such puissance shouldn't go unacknowledged by English teachers, who spend a great deal of their time helping students to extract value from stories and to discover the tremendous power of words and ideas.

Still, creating a screenwriting experience in the classroom may evoke a raised eyebrow or two. Whenever a catastrophe occurs, such as the Columbine High murders in 1999, parental and legislative fingers quickly point to the motion picture studios as being in part culpable. Critics lambaste a film such as *Basketball Diaries* because it contains a violent dream/drug sequence. The character played by Leonardo DiCaprio imagines that while wearing a trench coat and toting numerous assault weapons, he walks into school and methodically murders his classmates to the applause of his best friend. Similarly, in a scene in *The Matrix,* the character played by Keanu Reeves (who also sports a trench coat) walks into an office building while armed with a dozen or so weapons strapped to his body and one rather large bomb tucked into a briefcase. In slow motion, Reeves and his leather-clad girlfriend walk through the corridor, blowing the heads off the dozen or so police officers unfortunate enough to have been in the lobby when they arrived. Among others, former education secretary William Bennett has noted that it is beyond coincidence that Harris and Klebold donned trench coats and carried similar weaponry during their rampage at Columbine. And Bennett is probably right.

Certain films probably have the potential to steer impressionable adolescents toward acts of violence. However, there is also substantial evidence attesting to the influence of film upon building cultural sensitivity, influencing voting behavior, promoting enduring learning, changing erroneous perceptions, and other positive phenomena. Since the beginning of the twentieth century, a tiny cadre of innovators has always recommended that English teachers use film in the classroom. In 1915, Gerrish wrote, "Moving pictures everywhere will become a valuable adjunct in the mastery of skill in English composition" (p. 230). Teachers who ignore film not only fail to consider the most influential medium of our age, they also fail to capitalize on students' obvious proclivity for visual and auditory stimuli.

I ran the idea of a screenwriting project by Lina, a bright but lazy volleyball player in my freshman English class who managed to maintain an average hovering somewhere between 80 and 82 every grading period.

"Lina, what if I asked you to make a little movie in this class?" I asked.

"You don't make movies in English class," she looked at me, incredulous. "Besides, you don't have any cameras."

"I don't know. Maybe the coaches will let us borrow one or two of their old ones if we promise to take good care of them," I explained.

"Could be cool. Might be real cool. What would be the catch?"

"You'd have to write a screenplay," I said.

"Gotta have a script to make a movie. But, it's gotta be a great script," Lina said with some authority, as if she had lived on the backlot of a Hollywood studio her entire life. "Now, me. I could write a great script. I could write the world's best movie. How much money a guy make writing screenplays, Mr. B.?"

"Joe Esterhaus received a couple million for his last screenplay, I think."

"Good enough," Lina nodded. "Let's do it."

The Lure of Screenwriting

Perhaps it is not surprising that screenwriting is the most lucrative writing profession in the world today. Screenwriters make more than technical writers for Microsoft or Cisco, feature writers for the *New Yorker,* and certainly more than hopeful novelists. "Word for word, and dollar for dollar, you can make more money in screenwriting than in any other form of writing" (Hauge 1991, p. 267). Screenwriting has served as a rich uncle for writers for decades. William Faulkner, Aldous Huxley, Theodore Dreiser, Ring Lardner, John Steinbeck, Raymond Chandler, Richard Wright, Gore Vidal, Beth Henley, Arthur Miller, Edward Albee, Harold Pinter, Tennessee Williams, Neil Simon, Stephen King, James Michener, and others have written screenplays at one time or another. In 1939, F. Scott Fitzgerald supplemented his $33 royalty check from the sales of his books (that is, the total royalties from his book sales for the year amounted to thirty-three dollars) with a part-time screenwriting job that paid him $1,500 per week. In the 1980s, screenwriter and novelist William Goldman noted, "For the hardcover publication of my first novel, I was paid five thousand dollars. Such was the glory of its reception that, for my second novel, I was paid twenty-five hundred dollars. For *Harper,* my first Hollywood film, I received eighty thousand dollars" (1983, p. 74). Today, it is not uncommon for Hollywood producers to option screenplays at $1,000,000 a pop.

After I saw the enthusiasm with which even Lina embraced the idea of screenwriting, I wondered why it had taken me so long to understand what the vocational education teacher Frank seemed to readily comprehend. Students often perceive of reading and the study of words as archaic and thuddingly dull. A screenplay could allow students to break free of abstract language for a while. If I could hook students through a screenwriting experience, perhaps I could find a way to slip in some literature, writing instruction, guidelines for oral presentations, and other useful activities close to my heart.

Screenwriting Today

There is a good reason that more commercial movies are being produced and shot in America than at any other time in history (in 1998, approximately 550 films)— making a film has gotten progressively easier over the years. As the cost of cameras and editing equipment continues to decline, the motion picture industry promises to boom well into the century (Valenti 1999). While studio products represent a significant portion of new releases, independent films now account for two-thirds of all new releases and 95 percent of the direct-to-video market (American film Marketing Association 1999). Although attendance at movie theaters per capita has been declining since 1920, the proliferation of channels on cable television has ensured an ever-expanding marketplace for film. As the writer E. L. Doctorow has noted, "Films are so dominant now, as a force, and so important, and so instrumental in the way young people learn things . . . that I can see gifted young people finding it as easy and feasible to make a film as to write a story or first novel" (2000, p. 25).

In perusing how-to books on screenwriting, one rule is emphasized again and again—a screenwriter should use images, not words, as the basic units of communication. Spottiswood writes, "The director must constantly aim at the elimination of words" (1950, p. 24). Kazan comments, "You should be able to write a screenplay with virtually no words whatsoever—a sequence of images . . . tell the reader not only what they see, but how they feel about what they see" (1993, p. 248).

To demonstrate to students the superfluity of dialogue in film, I usually compare an excerpt from a film with the literary text from which it has been adapted. Any of the following pairs of novels/films would suffice, depending on the curriculum, availability of books, and a teacher's personal preferences. Table 4.1 contains some of my favorite pairs of films and novels.

Screenwriting for Students

Recently, I used the scene from Ray Bradbury's science fiction classic *Something Wicked This Way Comes* where the father first meets Mr. Dark in the town's library. In the book, while his son attempts to hide in the book stacks from Mr. Dark (the incarnation of the devil), the father attempts to fend off Dark's attack with wit and a belief in the power of good. Dark threatens the father and attempts to bribe him by offering him the chance to be young again in exchange for turning over his son. After some crisp dialogue heavy with nuance and allusions to the Bible and the works of Shakespeare and Milton, Dark threatens the father, then leaves. The chapter ends with some subtle, incisive observations about the bargains humans strike with themselves in life as they cope with their own longings and frailties.

In the film version, instead of merely asking the father to trade his youth for the life of his son, director Jack Clayton has Dark tear out pages from the Bible during their conversation. He teases the father by offering him the chance to relive life as a twenty-year-old. When the father does not respond to the bribe, Dark rips out a page, the page magically catches fire, and then Dark exclaims, "Twenty—gone!" then "twenty-five—gone!" until there is no more youth with which to bargain. When his repeated appeals to the father go unheeded, Dark grabs the father by the wrist and gives him "a taste of death." Through the use of some remarkable special effects, the father's arm begins to wrinkle then to putrefy as Dark's grip tightens. After seeing the film, most viewers will readily note that little of the initial text was kept for the film, and they will likely have no memory of the subtext and nuance of the scene from the book, either. In fact, in recollections of *Something Wicked This Way Comes,* most students will be unable to recall any part of the original chapter at all. Instead, they will remember from the film the withering arm and the pages of the Bible going up in flames.

Because students watch so much film, television, Internet video, and DVD/VHS outside of class, I rarely show more than a fifteen-minute clip from any

TABLE 4.1   Some Interesting Pairs of Books and Films

Book	Author	Film	Director
Blackboard Jungle (1954)	Evan Hunter	*Blackboard Jungle* (1957)	Richard Brooks
Bridge to Terabithia (1978)	Katherine Paterson	*Bridge to Terabithia* (1985)	Eric Till
Bright Lights, Big City (1985)	Jay McInerney	*Bright Lights, Big City* (1988)	James Bridges
Do Androids Dream of Electric Sheep? (1990)	Philip K. Dick	*Blade Runner*	Ridley Scott
Little Caesar (1929)	William Burnett	*Little Caesar* (1930)	Mervyn LeRoy
Macbeth	William Shakespeare	*Macbeth* (1948) *Macbeth* (1971) *Throne of Blood* (1957)	Orson Welles Roman Polanski Akira Kurosawa
Mildred Pierce (1941)	James Cain	*Mildred Pierce* (1945)	Michael Curtiz
Native Son (1940)	Richard Wright	*Native Son* (1950— available on video, stars Richard Wright as Bigger) *Native Son* (1986)	Jerrold Freedman
Play It as It Lays (1970)	Joan Didion	*Play It as It Lays* (1972)	Frank Perry
Romeo and Juliet	William Shakespeare	*Romeo and Juliet* (1968) *Romeo and Juliet* (1996)	Franco Zefferelli Baz Luhrmann
Sense and Sensibility	Jane Austen	*Sense and Sensibility* (1995)	Emma Thompson
Ship of Fools (1962)	Katherine Anne Porter	*Ship of Fools* (1965)	Stanley Kramer
Slaughterhouse Five (1969)	Kurt Vonnegut	*Slaughterhouse Five* (1972)	George Roy Hill
Something Wicked This Way Comes (1983)	Ray Bradbury	*Something Wicked This Way Comes* (1983)	Jack Clayton
Taming of the Shrew	William Shakespeare	*Ten Things I Hate About You* (1997)	Gil Junger
The Color Purple (1982)	Alice Walker	*The Color Purple* (1985)	Steven Spielberg
The Grapes of Wrath (1939)	John Steinbeck	*The Grapes of Wrath* (1940)	John Ford
The Milagro Beanfield War (1974)	John Nichols (1974)	*The Milagro Beanfield War* (1988)	Robert Redford
"The Swimmer" (1962) (in the collection of short stories called *The Brigadier and the Golf Widow*)	John Cheever	*The Swimmer* (1968)	Frank Perry

TABLE 4.1 *continued*

Book	Author	Film	Director
The Tempest	William Shakespeare	*Forbidden Planet* (1956)	Fred Wilcox
"The Tin Star" (1947), a short story from *No, But I Saw the Movie* (1983)	John Cunningham	*High Noon* (1952)	Fred Zinnemann
To Have and Have Not (1937)	Ernest Hemingway	*To Have and Have Not* (1944)	Howard Hawks
When the Legends Die (1963)	Hal Borland	*When the Legends Die* (1972)	Stuart Miller

film during class time. If students want to see an entire film, they can rent it at a video store or purchase it through the Internet.

Although students love participating in a unit on screenwriting, making a good film requires a student to do much hard, hard work. The student must listen intently, read critically, write clearly, speak expressively, and negotiate diplomatically. Despite the numerous intellectually challenging activities within the screenwriting experience, some students will relentlessly aim toward making what Frank feared most—a sort of MTV lip-sync reenactment of a favorite song starring themselves in the guises of their favorite rock, rap, or hip-hop stars. Although students who want to "go MTV" may certainly use MTV-style camerawork (quick cuts and severe close-ups) and appropriate music, the teacher must continually work to make sure students adhere to the requirements of the project—a story, a script, rich characterization, and innovative thinking about how to join image, sound, language, and literature. The objective of the screenwriting experience is to use students' proclivity for the image to get them immersed in using language for artistic and practical ends.

Over the past dozen or so years, I have altered aspects of the screenwriting experience to better fit my goals (student mastery of written and oral language, the ability to comprehend texts and make logical inferences, media literacy) as well as students' goals (have fun, be able to use equipment without "too much hassle," produce a video of lasting quality). One of the most gratifying side effects of the screenwriting experience is that students seem to become more critical of their own perceptions and values as they relate to popular culture. Having students work from the inside out by making their own video helps them to generate a new perspective on media and alerts them to the purposeful efforts of filmmakers, marketers, and advertisers to influence their values, dispositions, and spending habits.

I used to begin the screenwriting experience by giving lessons on various aspects of filmmaking—the format for a screenplay; the rudiments of good acting, camera angles, and editing—then setting students free to do their films. After receiving a few well-intentioned but poorly executed and very long films from students, I began requiring the completion of an initial, short film at the beginning of the project. If your students have not had much exposure to video, I suggest you begin with the mini–screenwriting unit (described in the first six days in the following sequence) in which the fundamentals of shooting, editing, acting, and writing are covered. If your students are already familiar with the format for scripts, know how to frame a shot effectively, are attuned to choreographing sound and image, and can position the camera so that it purposefully reflects a particular point of view, then they can skip this unit and jump right into the project on day seven. As you navigate through the screenwriting experience, keep in mind that the better student videos will share two traits:

(1) Their videos will have elicited some kind of emotional response in viewers.
(2) Their videos will revolve around the life of one central, sympathetic character.

Sequence of Activities

Day 1: Setting Up the Mini–Screenwriting Unit

When I asked students to get out a sheet of paper, I heard the groans again.
"Not again."
"No more writing, sir."
"This guy makes us write more essays than an encyclopedia has pages."
But when I moved over to an LCD projector that was hooked up to a VCR, students' faces brightened considerably.
"Cool, we're watching a movie, dude!"
"Hey, is this like a cartoon, Mr. B.?"
"Is this another ten-minute documentary?"
I said, "I'm going to play a clip from a film adaptation of *Romeo and Juliet* made in 1996. I want you to write down everything that you see and hear in this opening sequence. A lot is going to happen and you can't capture all of it. Just try to capture as much of it as you can. I'm going to play it twice, so anything you don't get the first time, maybe you'll get the second."
Although I do not particularly like the 1996 version of *Romeo and Juliet*, I use it because the interpretation is quite outrageous and most students have not seen it. I showed the opening eight to ten minutes to my class of ninth graders and asked them what they thought. Then I rewound it and played it again. Lina wrote the following description of the intro.

Setting for *Romeo and Juliet* (1996)
by Lina Fisher

Black, except for TV in center of the shot. News cast delivers the opening soliloquy.

Then, fast paced shots of Verona Beach, in California—1990's. Shots include buildings, people fighting, city streets and signs.

Shots then slow and introduce the Capulet Parents, Montague Parents, and other major characters.

Ends with more fast paced action shots. All the while loud unsettling music is played that evokes a feeling of desperation, like "something bad is going to happen."

Next, 3 Montague Boys riding in a car listening to hip-hop/techno music. Pull into gas station. Capulet boys are there. Words and threats are exchanged. Montague bites a thumb at Capulets. Guns pulled and more words.

Enter **TYBALT** (Capulet). Lights a cigarette, drops a lit match. More words exchanged (esp. between **TYBALT** and **BENVOLIO**). **TYBALT** draws gun and shooting ensues. **BENVOLIO** goes down (not shot) and lays in gasoline. Other Montague boys flee, one is shot in the car. **TYBALT** drops his cigarette and fire starts. **BENVOLIO** gets up and runs away. End scene with **TYBALT** walking away through the blaze.

After sharing some student responses, I gave students a handout of how Shakespeare described the scene (see Handout 4.1).

I chose the best, most dramatic readers to recite the passage aloud. When they finished, I asked students to try to discern what Shakespeare was trying to say.

"Do you think the director of the 1996 version of *Romeo and Juliet* altered Shakespeare's language? Could you tell? Do you remember? Should he have altered more of it? Do the passages say the same thing?"

Then I handed out the screenwriters' version (see Handout 4.2) and asked students to compare what they had written in their impromptu description of the scene with the screenwriters' version.

I asked students to discuss some of the differences among script, play, and their descriptions. Then I pointed out ways that students could have manipulated their impromptu reactions to the first scene so that they would fit the proper format for a screenplay. I handed out a half-page information sheet that concisely describes the format for a screenplay (Handout 4.3), which differs from the format of a play in important, but subtle ways.

"Think you could write a screenplay if I asked you?" I asked.

"No problem, Mr. B." At least, Lina seemed confident.

"How many of you have a camcorder at home that you think your parents would let you use for a school project?"

Four students raised their hands, not bad for a school who served families of modest means. "Okay, if you have access to a camcorder, ask your parents if you can bring it to school. If they will let you use it, bring your camcorders tomorrow."

HANDOUT **4.1**

From *Romeo and Juliet* by William Shakespeare

Prologue:
Two households, both alike in dignity,
In fair Verona, where we lay our scene,
From ancient grudge break to new mutiny,
Where civil blood makes civil hands unclean.
From forth the fatal loins of these two foes
A pair of star-cross'd lovers take their life;
Whose misadventured piteous overthrows
Do with their death bury their parents' strife.
The fearful passage of their death-mark'd love,
And the continuance of their parents' rage,
Which, but their children's end, nought could remove,
Is now the two hours' traffic of our stage;
The which if you with patient ears attend,
What here shall miss, our toil shall strive to mend.

Act One: Enter **SAMPSON** and **GREGORY**, of the house of Capulet, armed with swords and bucklers.

SAMPSON: Gregory, o' my word, we'll not carry coals.

GREGORY: No, for then we should be colliers.

SAMPSON: I mean, an we be in choler, we'll draw.

GREGORY: Ay, while you live, draw your neck out o' the collar.

SAMPSON: I strike quickly, being moved.

GREGORY: But thou art not quickly moved to strike.

SAMPSON: A dog of the house of Montague moves me.

GREGORY: To move is to stir; and to be valiant is to stand: therefore, if thou art moved, thou runn'st away.

SAMPSON: A dog of that house shall move me to stand: I will take the wall of any man or maid of Montague's.

GREGORY: That shows thee a weak slave; for the weakest goes to the wall.

SAMPSON: True; and therefore women, being the weaker vessels, are ever thrust to the wall: therefore I will push Montague's men from the wall, and thrust his maids to the wall.

GREGORY: The quarrel is between our masters and us their men.

SAMPSON: 'Tis all one, I will show myself a tyrant: when I have fought with the men, I will be cruel with the maids, and cut off their heads.

GREGORY: The heads of the maids?

SAMPSON: Ay, the heads of the maids, or their maidenheads; take it in what sense thou wilt.

GREGORY: They must take it in sense that feel it.

SAMPSON: Me they shall feel while I am able to stand: and 'tis known I am a pretty piece of flesh.

GREGORY: 'Tis well thou art not fish; if thou hadst, thou hadst been poor John. Draw thy tool! Here comes two of the house of the Montagues.

HANDOUT **4.2**

From the Script of *Romeo and Juliet* by Baz Luhrmann and Craig Pearce

EXT. HIGHWAY. AFTERNOON.
A ribbon of freeway stretching into a blue and pink late afternoon sky. A huge dark sedan, windows tinted gold, powers directly for us.
CUT TO: A heavy, low-slung pickup truck traveling toward the sedan.
WIDE SHOT: Sky, freeway, the cars closing.
TIGHT ON: The sedan.
TIGHT ON: The pickup.
Like thunderous, jousting opponents, the cars pass in a deafening cacophony of noise.
INT. TRUCK. AFTERNOON.
TIGHT ON: The fat face of **GREGORY**, yelling at the disappearing sedan.

GREGORY
A dog of the house of Capulet moves me!

He and the pimply-faced front-seat passenger, **SAMPSON**, explode with laughter. The red-haired driver, **BENVOLIO**, keeps his eyes on the road.

INT. TV STUDIO. DAY.

An **ANCHORWOMAN**; behind her, the faces of two middle-aged men. The caption reads, "Montague; Capulet. The feud continues." She speaks to the camera.

ANCHORWOMAN
Two households, both alike in dignity.
(In fair Verona, where we lay our scene)
From ancient grudge break to new mutiny,
Where civil blood makes civil hands unclean.

EXT. GAS STATION. AFTERNOON.

The truck is in the busy driveway of a large gas station, being filled with gas. The surrounding walls are painted with murals of blue sky and palm trees.

INT. TRUCK. AFTERNOON.

Inside the truck, **GREGORY** and **SAMPSON** are boasting outrageously. The driver's seat is empty.

> **GREGORY**
> I will take the wall of any man or maid of Capulets.

EXT. GAS STATION. AFTERNOON.

> **SAMPSON**
> I will show myself a tyrant.
> When I have fought with the men
> I will be civil with the maids,
> I will cut off their heads.

> **GREGORY**
> *(mock outrage)* The heads of the maids?

SAMPSON leers lecherously at a minibus full of Catholic schoolgirls next to them.

> **SAMPSON**
> Ay, the heads of the maids, or their maidenheads—
> Take it in what sense thou wilt.

> **GREGORY**
> They must take it in sense that feel it.

GREGORY and **SAMPSON** pump up the song on the sound system while gyrating crudely at the girls.

> **GREGORY/SAMPSON**
> *(singing)*
> I am a pretty piece of flesh!
> I am a pretty piece of flesh!
> Me, they shall feel while I am able to stand;
> I am a pretty piece of flesh!

EXT. GAS STATION–MINIMART. AFTERNOON.

The teacher nun from the minibus returns to the vehicle.

GREGORY'S P.O.V.: The girls' minibus pulls away, revealing . . . a tough-looking Latino boy, **ABRA,** leaning against the huge, dark sedan.

GREGORY suddenly stops gyrating.

CLOSE ON:

SAMPSON
Here comes the house of Capulet.

Source: Extracted from Baz Luhrmann and Craig Pearce, *William Shakespeare's* Romeo and Juliet: *The Contemporary Film, The Classic Play* (1996). New York: Random House.

After class, I called the football coaches. It was March and I knew that they wouldn't be using their camcorders much in spring drills. Also, the library had two or three camcorders. After two telephone calls and a little explaining, I had three more cameras in case we needed them.

Day 2: Setting Up Groups and Establishing a Common Purpose

The next class, four students brought in camcorders and a fifth was waiting on approval from his father, who was out of town on business (he worked on an oil rig in the Gulf of Mexico). I asked the four students who brought camcorders to serve as anchors for the screenwriting groups. Then I asked Lina to serve as custodian of one borrowed camcorder (from the coaches' office) and as anchor for the fifth group. Because successful screenwriting requires cooperation and cohesion, I allowed students to choose to join any of the five groups. Because I had twenty students in class, most groups had four members, though one had three and another had five. After I assessed the state of the groups (made sure that the groups

---

HANDOUT **4.3**

The Format for a Screenplay

In a screenplay, the name of the character is always in capital letters (even when the name is mentioned in the stage directions). Whenever a character speaks, the name is centered on the page. To write dialogue, indent about ten spaces from the left margin and single-space. Place the dialogue directly under the name of the character speaking (skip no lines). Directions for the action and setting are written in all capital letters flush left. Two lines should be skipped between dialogue and directions for action and setting.

were solid, not too many creative types in a single group), I asked students to decide upon these roles: director/editor, cameraperson, screenwriter, and lead actor/actress. Although everyone in the group would have to write, read, speak, act, film, and negotiate at different times, these roles were a necessary distribution of power to ensure that everything was done properly.

Next, I asked students to write a list of five to ten of their favorite films of all time.

My Favorite Movies
by Lina Fisher

Braveheart

Natural Born Killers

Romy and Michelle's High School Reunion

Lost Highway

Trainspotting

The Sixth Sense

Monty Python's Holy Grail

The Usual Suspects

You should have no difficulty getting students to discuss their favorite films. After I learned the titles of some offbeat films I never knew existed, I asked students to identify commonalities among the films mentioned within their group.

"Look at the favorite film lists among your group members. Is there a particular genre, theme, setting, or character type that is evident among all members of the group? What kind of themes or characters are dominant?"

Then, I pushed them to come to a consensus about their preferences in films. "I want the individual who has been chosen as screenwriter to write a brief paragraph describing each member's preferences in movies and the similarities (if any) among group members. If you haven't yet selected a screenwriter, this is a good time to do so."

The remainder of the day was taken up with a demonstration of camcorder technique. I encouraged students to use many close-ups and to frame scenes toward a particular purpose.

"For example, if the purpose is to make a character seem helpless or weak, the cameraman might shoot down on the subject." I asked Lina to sit on the floor and to look sad and helpless. I hopped onto a chair and pointed the camera down at her. She frowned, then scowled at me.

"This shot could make Lina look powerless. If the purpose is to make a character seem strong, the camera might shoot up at the character from ground level."

I changed places with Lina. She stood on the chair and I sat on the floor and pointed the camera up at her. She gave me her best flexed muscle pose and smiled.

In general, students who are new to camcorders tend to stand too far away from their subjects when they film, don't shoot enough footage, and are too jittery with the camera. The microphone attached at the front of the camcorder is usually not particularly sensitive—another reason to stress close-ups and louder, more theatrical voices.

"No stick people in your videos. That means, I do not want anybody to shoot from too far away. If you shoot from too far away, everyone looks like a stick. Shoot close-ups. Now I want the cameraman in each group to take some close-ups of all the others in the group engaging in a conversation. I want the individuals being filmed to talk and I want to be able to hear the conversation."

As I walked around the room, I corrected students who were speaking too softly and cameramen who were too timid about getting into people's faces.

"Directors and cameramen, take this video home and watch and listen to it. See how well the microphone picked up sound and how effectively you shot the close-ups."

At the end of the period, I handed each member of each group copies of three different short stories I had taken from *Sudden Fiction* (Shapard and Thomas, 1987), *Micro Fiction* (Stern, 1996), and a few magazines. That is, for a group of four, I made twelve copies. Each member received three stories. In another group, I handed each member of the group three different sets of stories. With the incredible number of great stories available, I see no need to limit students to the same stories. I asked group members to read all the stories and to decide which story would make the best film.

Day 3: Deciding on a Story

I handed each student the appropriate number of "prospectus" worksheets (to match the number of stories they were considering) (see Handout 4.4) and said, "Today is reading day. I want you to read all the short stories for your group. Fill out this "prospectus" for each story. After everyone in the group has read all the stories, discuss and rate the attractiveness of each, including in your discussion how each story might be adapted for film. Remember that you can change any aspect of the story—characters, setting, themes, plot—to fit a particular purpose. For example, the setting of a story in a sixteenth-century castle might be changed to a twenty-first-century high school."

I asked groups to give me an indication of what story they intended to adapt by the beginning of the class period the following day. Because their future endeavors hinged upon the story they selected, students read the stories closely and critically. If some groups finished reading early and decided upon a story unanimously, I allowed them to begin discussing the changes they would have to make to accommodate their meager equipment, limited props, and the impending due date.

HANDOUT **4.4**

Prospectus for a Video

Names of main characters, physical/emotional description, and personalities:

_____

_____

_____

_____

_____

Brief summary of plot:

_____

_____

_____

_____

_____

Setting:

_____

_____

_____

_____

_____

Attractive aspects of story for adaptation:

_____

_____

_____

_____

_____

Negative aspects of story for adaptation:

_____

_____

_____

_____

_____

_____

Possibilities:

_____

_____

_____

_____

_____

_____

Days 4 and 5: Learning the Art of the Screen Adaptation

I asked students to agree on the short story they would adapt. I handed out the evaluation criteria for the adaptation and went over it (see Handout 4.5).

"Everyone needs to turn in a working script and a video on Monday. Get busy today on writing the screenplay in the appropriate format. Spend the remainder of today and all of tomorrow planning, rehearsing, and filming." Lina's group decided to adapt a short story by Stephen Dixon from *Sudden Fiction* called "The Signing." Because Lina was the most vocal supporter for doing "The Signing," her group allowed her to write the screenplay. An excerpt follows.

HANDOUT **4.5**

Evaluation for the Adaptation of the Short Story

    a. Script—Appropriately formatted, grammatically correct (except for purposeful slang), compellingly written—50 points
    b. Film—Quality of camerawork (no stick people, no jittery images, good framing), sound (audible), artistry—50 points

The Signing
by Lina Fisher,
based on the short story by Stephen Dixon (from Sudden Fiction*)*

INT. HOSPITAL CORRIDOR—3rd Floor
An empty white, sterile hall. **MAN** leaves a room on the left and walks down the hall with blank expression. **NURSE** leaves the room after **MAN** and runs to catch him.

> **NURSE**
> Are you going to make arrangements for the deceased?

> **MAN**
> No.

> **NURSE**
> What do you want done with the body, then?

> **MAN**
> Burn it.

> **NURSE**
> But we don't do that here.

> **MAN**
> Give it to science.

> **NURSE**
> You'll need to sign some papers.

> **MAN**
> Give them to me.

> **NURSE**
> They'll take a while. You could wait in the guest lounge.

> **MAN**
> Can't. No time for that.

> **NURSE**
> And her belongings?

They come to an elevator across from an unmanned nurse's station. **MAN** rings for it.

> **MAN**
> I have to go.

> **NURSE**
> You can't!

> MAN
> I am.
>
> The elevator comes. **MAN** steps inside.
>
> NURSE
> Wait!
>
> The door closes. **NURSE** runs back down the hall.
>
> NURSE
> Doctor!

Day 6: Presenting the Mini-adaptations

Most groups were ready at the beginning of class, although one group said that they needed one more day. I allowed them to play their videos the following day (we could probably fit only four videos in one day, anyway), but told them, "Because I'm giving you an extra day, I'm expecting your script and video to be better than those we'll see today."

Before commencing, I handed out several copies of the criteria for "evaluation for the adaptation of the short story" (Handout 4.5, the same sheet that I used to grade their videos). Then I asked students to comment upon and rate all the videos of their peers on one evaluation sheet. After they had seen all of the videos, I asked them to rank the videos from best to worst. Students were not allowed to rate their own video.

"Please keep in mind that each group had to write and film this story very quickly. Give at least one kudo and at least one suggestion for improvement. This short video is the 'practice video' for the next assignment, 'the big production.' As you present your video, do not preface it by saying anything. Just play it. Afterwards, you can field any questions that classmates might have and describe what lessons you learned."

Four groups showed their videos and we discussed what they had learned about screenwriting and the art of film.

"How do you make titles?"

"We tried to stick to the script, but found that we ad-libbed a lot."

"You had to scream for the microphone to pick up your voice."

Day 7: Getting Ready for the Big Production

To start the day, the late group played their video, a shoddy MTV-type video in which the students climbed on the roof of a house and played air guitars and drums (actually trash cans) to AC/DC's oldie, "Shot Down in Flames." I walked over to the VCR, pressed Stop, and asked, "Is there a story here or is this just a rendition of a song?"

"Sir, it gets better. Aaron falls off the roof."

"Yeah, it's hilarious, dude."

I smiled and said, "No MTV-style films. I said that at the beginning. No credit. Class, get out your evaluations and rate the four videos you saw yesterday from best to worst. You may not rate your own."

I took up the assessments and added up what students considered the best and worst of the bunch. To my surprise, the class favorite was not Lina's group's weird adaptation of "The Signing," but an avant-garde adaptation of Philip O'Connor's "Gerald's Song" (also in *Sudden Fiction*). Although I asked them not to rate it, students voted the limp AC/DC tribute as the worst, anyway. I added up the scores and gave the members of the group that did "Gerald's Song" four packs of peanut M&Ms (to be eaten during class or after school only).

I suggested reconstituting new groups for the big video. However, most of the students liked their groups and wanted them to remain intact for the big production. So, of their own volition, two individuals in the AC/DC group asked if they could join one of the other groups. Then Sydeana, a quiet A student on the girls' volleyball team (with Lina), asked if she could form a new, separate group with Lina. Lina's group did not want her to leave, but Sydeana and Lina obviously had something in mind for their big production, so the group eventually relented. The two remaining members of AC/DC joined Lina's former group. So, although an old group died, a new group was formed. The number of groups remained at five.

As with Lina and Sydeana, sometimes one or two persons in a group have particularly vivid visions of what they would like to accomplish in a video. I always allow such impassioned individuals to break off from their group at this point. Anytime students show initiative and enthusiasm for a difficult project, I always think it best to give them a chance.

Once the groups were settled, I went over the evaluation sheet for the "big production." (See Handout 4.6.)

Because film is more about the visual experience than the writing (and because everything I do except the big production is weighted toward writing), I weigh the film more heavily than the script. If I weighed the script more heavily than the film, then students could possibly produce an awful video and a brilliant script. Like film studios, I wanted the final product to count more than the inputs. As they did with their short productions, students filled out a prospectus for at least two ideas for the big production. I requested that at least one idea involve adapting scenes from a favorite novel. A second idea could involve writing an original screenplay. The big production would be a short film, not less than five minutes or longer than twenty.

I asked, "How many times in your life do you get the opportunity to see an idea come to life? This is your chance. If you have an idea for a screenplay or if you have ever read a book that you think should have been made into a movie, this is your chance to do it. I urge you to lobby your group on behalf of your idea."

As students discussed their ideas, I circulated around the room. As I listened to students, I tried to pay particular attention to the feasibility of their projects within the absurdly short time frame that I had given them.

HANDOUT **4.6**

Evaluation for "The Big Production," a Film of 5–20 Minutes

Remember that one page of screenplay usually translates to one minute on the screen.

I. Script, 25 points
   A. Proper screenplay format
   B. Quality of writing (correct usage and spelling, realistic dialogue, three-dimensional characters)
   C. Plot (keeps the audience's attention, adheres to its own rules)
   D. Creativity
   E. Notebooks (students compile all the activities, drafts, and revised copies, location notes, and anything else and organize them in a notebook)
II. Film, 75 points
   A. Purposeful and effective camerawork
   B. Audible and appropriate sound
   C. Music and sound effects contribute to the themes of the screenplay
   D. Artistically rendered
   E. Well produced—titles at beginning and end, smooth transitions, decent editing (☺)

I said, "You have about a week to conceptualize, write, and film your movie, so keep it fairly simple. However, do not underestimate what you can accomplish. After all, Orson Welles wrote, shot, and completed his film of *Macbeth* in twenty-one days."

From the conversations in the room, I could hear that in most groups, students were actively campaigning for their ideas. As they argued, I thought to myself, "How pleasant it is to have students fighting over the right to lead and work on an academic project!"

Day 8: Defining the Character

To begin, I asked students to briefly describe the story that they would film. Then I asked the screenwriter in each group to the write a one-sentence summary of the project. For example, Lindsey and Jennifer, who decided to adapt a novel, wrote, "We are going to film an adaptation of parts of *Bridge to Terabithia* using two of our friends in the lead roles." Lina and Sydeana, the volleyball girls who joined together to film their big idea, wrote, "Sydeana has an idea for a screenplay about what it would be like if men could menstruate. We're going to make a film about that."

Once students explained their story ideas, I asked them to begin working on the characters who would inhabit their screenplays. I said, "Each student in the group must create one to four characters. In a brief character sketch (an informative–descriptive piece), give some idea about the character's height, weight, usual type of dress, friends, job, hobbies, mannerisms, aspirations, political beliefs, habits, favorite song; the way she/he sits, walks and talks; the place she/he calls home."

Once the creativity began rolling, one student's ideas fired another's imagination, and the ideas continued to build, especially in the early going. When they were done, I asked students to read some of their character descriptions aloud. Sydeana wrote the following character sketch about Josh, the main character in their film about men menstruating.

Character Sketch of "Josh"
by Sydeana Martin

Josh is a college senior at Florida State University. He is well liked by his friends, quite handsome, and is dating a pretty and popular girl. He's got dark hair and blue eyes, is about 6'2," and was a basketball player in high school, but he was more concerned with his grades than sports at FSU, so now he's only on the court with his friends Bill and Ted. He's a computer science major, planning to enter the workforce as soon as he graduates (no grad school plans). He also hopes to have a family, and some days he wishes he could forget about making a living so he could spend more time at home.

Josh works at a cool little pizza restaurant where he serves and cooks during the afternoon lunch rush. After work, he usually goes by the mall and walks around. He really likes Dave Matthews, Sarah McLachlan, and sometimes hip hop. He's most afraid of failing as a man, or making a mistake, whatever the mistake may be. He isn't as sure of himself as he would like to be, or as others imagine him to be. He likes peanut butter and jelly sandwiches for lunch, just like a grammar school kid. His favorite movie is *Ferris Bueller's Day Off*, although he has no idea why.

There are many things that Josh hates and loves. He loves dogs, his university, his girlfriend, and technology. He loves his sports-utility vehicle and the town he grew up in, his grandmother's pecan pie and his grandfather's collection of rifles. He hates some stuff too. He hates ticks, cats, people who drive too slow, people who drive too fast, and his great uncle Mervin (the family drunk). He really hates the fact that he believes he loves his girlfriend more than she loves him. Josh thinks he would like to get married one day, but his girlfriend wants to finish with grad school and have a job before she takes any kind of step like that.

Day 9: Making the Main Character Distinctive

I began class by reiterating that most successful screenplays involve stories that take the perspective of a single character. I asked, "Who are some characters that you remember from yesterday? Who are some memorable characters from literature? What makes a character memorable?"

I tried to lead the discussion on character so that students would conclude that a memorable character is one who might be distinctive physically (Cyrano's nose, Zorro's mask, Captain Hook, the "one-armed man" from *The Fugitive*) or in speech or mannerisms (the Southern drawl of Forrest Gump, the meticulous manners of Ashley Wilkes, the encyclopedic knowledge of Sherlock Holmes). In collaboration with other members of the group, I asked the designated screenwriter to consider the setting and opening scenes.

"Where does the opening scene take place? What is the main character doing? Why is he doing it? I want you to come in tomorrow with a sketch of the opening scene."

Day 10: Writing the Prequel and Deciding on a Prop

I asked each group to read their opening scene aloud. Students and I asked questions as they occurred to us. After all groups had presented, I made the next assignment.

"Now I want you to write a prequel for the main character in the twenty-four-hour period *before* the screenplay opens. Write this as a narrative (not a script) and follow the conventions for effective writing. With every prequel, I want you to furnish a prop that is representative of your main character. Remember in *Catcher in the Rye*, Holden Caulfield wore his father's old red hunting cap. In *To Kill a Mockingbird*, Scout had a treasure box. You can draw or paint something if you don't want a physical prop. You need to write the prequel and show your prop to the rest of class tomorrow."

Day 11: Presentation of Character Sketch and Props; Deciding on a Shooting Schedule

Students do amazing things with prequels and props. For example, Jennifer and Lindsey created a motivational device for the actor playing the part of Leslie in their adaptation of *Bridge to Terabithia* (see Figure 4.1). Other students brought in artifacts such as a blue bandanna, a necklace, and a blanket. One group whose main character was a juvenile delinquent brought in an old black-and-white photo of a group member's grandparents.

"These are Ned's grandparents. His mom was a stripper, so he asked her parents to raise him. They tried, but the Child Protective Agency found out and took him away. Then, he went into foster homes."

Students read their twenty-four-hour prequels aloud and explained how their works of art represented the main character. When they were finished, I said, "I want you to notice how filmmakers often change scenes and settings to keep the action lively, so I am going to show you the first fifteen minutes from *Romeo and Juliet* again. I want you to write down the number of *locations* that the cameramen had to use in this fifteen-minute opening."

I showed the clip. Students identified eight locations used in the first fifteen minutes of the film—a television set, a convenience store/gas station, a police pull-over on a busy street, Romeo on the beach, the prince in a steam room, Romeo

FIGURE 4.1   **Motivational Device for Actors**
              in Adaptation of *Bridge to Terabithia*

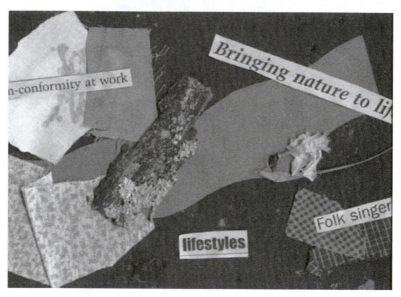

and Benvolio at a billiards hall, the Capulet house getting ready for a party, and a group of the Montagues on the beach at night.

"Now I want you to sketch out the locations for each of the major scenes in your film. Once you figure out what locations you will use, you might want to shoot all the scenes at a particular location at once, then go back and put the scenes in the correct sequence during the editing process."

Some cinematographers try to imbue locations with particular colors and tones. Cinematographer Walton writes, "One of the first things I like to do, and I imagine it's frequently done, is to take a film, more or less scene by scene, and try to picture what it would be like just in terms of the color palette" (1983, p. 373). Sydeana, the independent girl who broke away from her group to write a screenplay with Lina, wrote the following descriptions for the locations for her scenes.

Breakdown of Scenes

Scene one: indoor party scene at Josh's apartment, bright colors, loud

Scene two: inside a grocery store, sterile, fluorescent lighting

Scene three: indoors at a political rally in an office building, red, white and blue

Scene four: inside, during dinner at Frank's apartment, somber grays

In the past, I required that students write a few sentences with regard to plot and location on index cards, but the more I required it, the more students seemed to resist the idea. Until recently, using index cards was standard operating procedure for screenwriters—index cards can slip into a pocket and can easily be rearranged and revised. However, over time, I learned that students found index cards too confining. Apparently, many successful screenwriters share students' disdain for the index card format and have opted for a more authentic, spontaneous approach. For example, Luis Valdez, screenwriter of *Zoot Suit* and *La Bamba*, writes, "I don't work from index cards or an outline, I work up pages. And I keep everything from scraps and I put them all together into a binder, two binders, three binders, whatever it takes. Usually there's a binder of research stuff, apart from books; a fat book of notes; another binder of notes I've written with respect to character; finally there's the binder from which I begin to write scenes" (1993, p. 13). So now, I usually require students to keep everything that they use in their filming—notes, index cards, scraps of paper—in a notebook. I want to see the progression of their ideas and work over time. At the end of the project, the notebook sometimes provides a better documentation of the work that went into a video than the finished video itself.

Days 12 and 13: Writing the Screenplay

I opened the day by asking students to get out all their materials. "I am going to give you the next two days to write your screenplay and shoot your video. You may begin now. If you have to leave the classroom to shoot a sequence, you must first show me your completed script, indicate what location you need, and ask my permission to leave the room. No more than two groups may leave at any time. You may not disturb any other class, be overly loud, or wander the halls aimlessly. You may want to do all your shooting after school. Two days from now, I'll show you how to edit. For now, you should concentrate on writing a good screenplay and mapping out when and how you'll shoot each scene. Any questions?"

After I answered a few queries, I continued, "As you write, I'm going to walk around the room and check your notebooks. Please get out all the materials you have gathered thus far in the screenwriting experience—the favorite films list, video, and script from the mini–screenwriting unit; the description of the setting of *Romeo and Juliet*; the brief character sketch; the twenty-four-hour prequel and prop for the main character; and the descriptions of locations/settings (on index cards or papers in a notebook)." Then I walked around and checked to make sure that every group had a substantial amount of material from which to work. Because no one had a completely finished script, most student discussion centered on the script, when they could meet after school, and the prospective locations they planned to use.

Screenwriting guru Syd Field (1981, pp. 73–94) suggests that a film should somehow communicate the nature of the conflict and introduce the main character within the first few minutes of the film. As students write their scripts and shoot their videos, I continually remind them of the following points:

- Most effective films proceed from the perspective of a main character with whom the audience can empathize.
- Voice should be audible; camera angle should be purposeful.
- Setting, plot, dialogue, and characterization are negotiable. For example, if a piece of dialogue seems out of character or preposterous, it is the duty of the group to rewrite it to better fit the situation.

Days 14 and 15: Editing and Adding Sound

Although many groups will not have finished shooting all their footage, at this point you should demonstrate the fundamentals of editing. I usually set up at least three simple editing suites in class. The basic editing suite consists of two VCRs and a monitor. Students need to be careful that they do not damage the master tape—the tape containing all their raw video footage. Some groups make a copy of the master right away. Editing tapes is not difficult—you press Play on one machine while you press Record on the other—but you should notify students that most VCRs begin by going in reverse for a few frames, and it usually takes a few frames more before an image appears. So, students should give sufficient lag time before and after a piece of film to ensure that nothing gets cut off. If you have access to real video editing equipment, or if you own some of the new, inexpensive computer editing software, or if your school has a media department with students who can help with editing and dubbing, then this last paragraph is meaningless to you. You have no choice but to use the equipment available to you. If, like me, you are a teacher who has access to only one computer (which doesn't work), then you can go the cheapie route and hook up some VCRs and monitors.

Again, I reminded students that their video would be judged upon the criteria specified on the evaluation sheet. "In editing, make sure that you have titles at the beginning and the end and make the transitions between scenes as smooth as possible. For titles, you can shoot a piece of notebook paper with the title written on it or you can write titles on the chalkboard and shoot that. Be creative. You don't have to use fancy gear to have a title."

Novelist and screenwriter Richard Price has noted that "[t]he only scripts that don't get tampered with are scripts that don't get made" (1993, p. 83). Students should revise their scripts to match the content of their video. In other words, on-the-set changes must be logged and rewritten into the script.

During the editing process, many groups discovered that they needed further film footage. In particular, some groups forgot to include reaction shots of the main character. The editing sequence is a good time to add reaction shots or to include new shots that are needed to make the video coherent. Allen says, "Editing is not taking out, it's putting together. It's taking a story, which has been photographed from many different angles and, very often, in many different takes, and making it play in the best possible way that it can" (1983, p. 382).

Part of the requirement for the video is that students add music or sound effects. If the VCRs or camcorders you have do not allow audio dubbing, then students may want to record sound effects and music separately on a cassette recorder.

Composer David Grusin advises that "the function of a score is subliminal and psychological. What we try to accomplish in film scoring is to channel . . . responses in an organized way, so that an audience can be moved in one direction or another without actually knowing why" (1983, p. 387).

Days 17 and 18: Presentation of Final Videos

On presentation day, I advised students not to preface their films with any words or stories. Instead, they should simply show the films and allow their fellow students to evaluate their quality. I suggest handing out several "big production" evaluation sheets so students can rate each video (except their own). They should rate only the film component of the evaluation. As teacher, I rated both the film and the script.

Day 19: Writing a Post-Video Paper

After I have given prizes to most participants in the groups who produced worthy videos and solid scripts, I asked students to write one of the following: .

  a. A narrative describing something that happened during the process of shooting the video
  b. A critical analysis of the differences between print and film
  c. A prognostication on the future of print or film
  d. A short story describing some escapades of the group during filming

Then, I handed out the assessment sheet for the post-video paper (Handout 4.7) and went over it.

H A N D O U T   4.7

Evaluation for the Post-Video Paper

  1. Content, 34 points
     Narrative/short story—Do you tell a good story from a consistent point of view?
     Analysis/prognostication—Do you offer specific evidence and show depth of insight?
  2. Style, 33 points
     Varied sentence structure, appropriate voice, impressive vocabulary, awareness of sentence rhythm, well-organized, strong closing.
  3. Punctuation and Grammar, 33 points
     Proper use of periods, commas, quotation marks, and semicolons; capitalization; precise language.

The Value of Screenwriting

Screenwriting is one of the most enjoyable experiences most students will have in secondary school. Not only do they get the opportunity to express themselves in visual and auditory terms, they collaborate with their friends on creating a work of art. Some students who would never speak up during discussions of composition and literature blossom during the screenwriting experience. As a teacher, you get to use the video as an excuse to have students read short stories or novels with an intensely critical eye, write numerous papers, and learn something about media literacy from the inside out. Ten or twenty years after students graduate from high school, a student or a teacher will be able to pop a cassette into the VCR and view a video testimonial to adolescent life in the early twenty-first century. Sure beats a worksheet on adverbial clauses.

Sydeana and Lina, the independent filmmakers, wrote a bitingly funny, interesting script, "If Men Could Menstruate." I offer one scene (of five) for your reading pleasure.

Act One, Scene One

Scene One is set in Tallahassee, Florida, a small college town, at a party on a warm Friday night in June. The opening scene takes place at **JOSH'S** apartment. Camera takes a close-up view of **JOSH**, **JOHN**, and **BILL** who are sitting on an old, plaid couch. **JOSH** speaks first while holding a bottle of Coors Light in his left hand.

JOSH
Man, you guys just don't understand. My flow was so strong.
I went through a whole pack of Always in one week!

Camera takes a close-up of **JOHN** and **BILL**.

JOHN AND BILL
Dude!

JOSH
And you guys do know that sex is always better
during that time of the month.

JOHN and **BILL** agree adamantly, making movements and noises indicating their firm belief in **JOSH'S** statement.

BILL
Yeah! I can always pump more iron when I'm menstruating.

JOHN
It's great being a man!

JOHN holds up his beer.

                        JOHN
        Let's have a toast. To men and their power to menstruate.

JOSH and BILL hold up their hands to toast.

                    JOSH AND BILL
                      Here, here!

FRANK walks up to JOSH, JOHN, and BILL. Camera includes all four characters.

                        FRANK
              I couldn't help but overhear you guys.
            Really, though, if you think that's something,
              my menstruation lasts seven whole days.

JOSH takes a swig of beer and looks unbelievably at FRANK.

                        JOSH
              Man, you are such a showoff!
        You're always bragging about how long and how much.
                    Give us a break.

Camera pans out to take a wider shot. Moving into JOSH'S space, FRANK points his
finger at JOSH'S face.

                        FRANK
        Are you calling me a liar, you lily-white pansy?
        I bet you didn't even start your period until last year.
        Of course, we can always just ask your girlfriend about that.

JOSH jumps up from the couch and goes for FRANK'S face. They struggle a little before
JOSH and BILL separate them.

                        BILL
              Come on you two. Knock it off.

JEANNA and CATHY walk up about this time. They make faces to show their disgust.

                        JEANNA
            Can't you guys talk about anything else?
                  I mean, it's so gross.

                        CATHY
        I agree. It's all Frank ever talks about.

> **JOSH**
> You girls are just jealous because you can't menstruate.
>
> **BILL**
> There's a word for that. I think it's called "menses-envy."
>
> **JEANNA**
> Thanks, professor Bill for that bit of useless information.
> Come on Cathy. Let's go get some burgers.
>
> **CATHY**
> These guys are so moody.
> It must be all those hormones in their system.
>
> **JEANNA** and **CATHY** walk away. Camera focuses on **JOSH** and **FRANK** who are still facing each other.
>
> **FRANK**
> Man, I'm sorry. I shouldn't have jumped down your throat.
> It's just that a guy gets a little defensive when you question his menstruation.
> It's like questioning his manhood.
>
> **JOSH**
> You're right. I was only kidding around. Hey!
> Everyone knows you are a three-pad man.
>
> They hug in a "manly" way. Camera fades out.

REFERENCES

Allen, D. Interview by W. Goldman. In Goldman, W. (1983). *Adventures in the Screen Trade*. New York: Dell, 382–386.

American Film Marketing Assocation (1999). The economic consequences of independent film making. Available at *http://www.afma.com/*.

Doctorow, E. L. (2000, Winter). "Mangled at the Movies." *Authors Guild Bulletin*, 19–33.

Field, S. (1981). *Screenplay: The Foundations of Screenwriting*. New York: Dell.

Gerrish, C. (1915, April). "The Relation of Moving Pictures to English Composition." *English Journal*, 226–230.

Goldman, W. (1983). *Adventures in the Screen Trade*. New York: Dell.

———. (2000). *Which Lie Did I Tell? More Adventures in the Screen Trade*. New York: Pantheon.

Grusin, D. Interview by W. Goldman. In Goldman, W. (1983). *Adventures in the Screen Trade*. New York: Dell, 386–391.

Hauge, M. (1991). *Writing Screenplays That Sell*. New York: Harper Perennial.

Kazan, N. Interview. In Schanzer, K., and Wright, T., eds. (1993). *American Screenwriters*. New York: Avon Books, 243–256.

Marcus, F., ed. (1971). *Film and Literature: Contrast in Media*. London: Chandler.

Pelham, J., ed. (1998). *Suddenly*. Houston: Martin House.

Price, R. Interview. In Schanzer, K., and Wright, T., eds. (1993). *American Screenwriters.* New York: Avon Books, 75–96.

Shapard, R., and Thomas, J. (1987). *Sudden Fiction.* Salt Lake City, UT: Gibbs-Smith.

Spottiswood, R. (1950). *A Grammar of the Film.* Berkeley: University of California Press.

Stern, J. (1996). *Micro Fiction.* New York: W. W. Norton.

Valdez, L. Interview. In Schanzer, K., and Wright, T., eds. (1993). *American Screenwriters.* New York: Avon Books, 1–18.

Valenti, J. (1999, May 4). C-Span broadcast of the congressional hearings on youth and violence.

Walton, T. Interview by W. Goldman. In Goldman, W. (1983). *Adventures in the Screen Trade.* New York: Dell, 372–377.

OUTCOMES

1. Students learned the rudiments of screenwriting.

2. Students wrote volumes of papers without whining.

3. Students worked together to create a work of art that was meaningful and original.

4. Students learned media literacy from the inside out.

5. Students worked on dramatic interpretation and oral delivery.

6. Students enjoyed writing and filming.

7. Students appreciated the lengthy, transformative process of moving from page to screen (and back).

ACTIVITIES

1. Read an excerpt from *Something Wicked This Way Comes* by Ray Bradbury.

2. Show the corresponding film clip from *Something Wicked This Way Comes.*

3. Discuss the various interpretations of Shakespeare's *Romeo and Juliet* (including Russian, Japanese, and contemporary versions).

4. Have students write a description of the setting for the subsequent film.

5. Show the opening fifteen minutes of the 1996 version of *Romeo and Juliet.*

6. Have students read their descriptions of the setting aloud.

7. Discuss the extent to which the 1996 version of *Romeo and Juliet* remained faithful to Shakespeare's language and plot.

8. Hand out copies of the film script that depict the first fifteen minutes of screen time.

9. Discuss the differences among script, play, and student descriptions.

10. Show students the correct format for a screenplay. Stimulate interest in screenwriting.

11. Place students in groups of four to five. These roles are essential to the success of shooting a video: director/editor, cameraperson, screenwriter, actor/actress, sound.

12. Have students list their favorite films. Have students identify similarities/differences within their group.

13. Show students how to operate camcorders. Emphasize close-ups and audible dialogue.

14. Allow students to play with camcorder to become familiar with its operation.

15. Hand out a variety of short stories to each group. Each group chooses one short story to adapt for video. Students alert teacher to the choice of the group. Students must turn in accompanying script with completed video.

16. Go over how videos and scripts will be evaluated.

17. Students shoot videos, then present them in class.

18. Students rate each others' videos and discuss what they learned during the process of adaptation (from story to video).

19. Students choose to write an original story or do an adaptation of a novel. Go over the evaluation criteria for the longer video.

20. Students write a character sketch of at least the main character. They decide upon at least one prop that is associated with the character.

21. Students create an opening scene—setting, action, tone, and time period may be established with this scene.

22. Students write a prequel for the main character twenty-four hours prior to the opening of the film.

23. Students present their character sketches to class and show props.

24. Students again watch the opening fifteen minutes of the 1996 version of *Romeo and Juliet,* noting the different locations used.

25. Students sketch out the locations that will be used in their adaptations.

26. Students write the screenplay and create a short video.

27. Students edit the video and enhance the sound.

28. Students present their videos.

29. Students evaluate videos.

30. Students write post-video papers on the process of adaptation and the move from words to images.

5 Novel Expectations

An experience encompassing the entire school year, wherein students elevate personal and peer expectations, develop themselves as critical readers, and author novels for publication—yes, novels

TIME: Usually runs over the course of a full school year

Background

It was around the first part of my third year of teaching that I began to contemplate assigning my students the task of writing a novel. I have always been a big proponent of cooperative learning, and it seemed to me that, if I could put together a reliable group, this project could be fun. At this point, though, I was merely playing with the idea, assessing what skills could be addressed and imagining the types of problems that could arise with such an extensive project. I knew that in my current setting—teaching six low-level ninth-grade English classes—it was not a very practical idea . . . unless, of course, I was willing to suspend all other work for the entire year and have students spend each day writing bits and pieces during class in the hopes of producing a major work of fiction. Homework was not a big priority with most of my students, and if I were to attempt having them write novels, it would need to be an entirely out-of-class assignment. It was tempting, though, to run it through at least one of my classes, simply because I knew the department chair as a teacher from the "old school," a volatile grammarian who spent an abundance of time dictating the specifics of what she felt each of her English teachers should be teaching during any given week, and that a project such as collaborative novels, an assignment that abandoned the tried-and-true pointlessness of an unyielding, unproductive tradition, an assignment that mocked the sacred five-paragraph essay, and gave only vague objectives that amounted to little among the ever-increasing state-mandated curriculum standards, would cause her at least a week of sleeplessness and stress. I fully expected her to confront me—concerned, but "willing to be open-minded"—at which time she would, no doubt, reeducate me on the need for accountability and teamwork in an English department that had no shortage of willing applicants. It was tempting, but at the time I knew it would not have been fair to those students who were still struggling to write complete sentences. Of course, there was my one ninth-grade English Honors class. . . .

In the end, I shelved the novel idea for that year. I was planning a move for the following year, and there were still too many details to work out before I could justify implementing such an ambitious project. I had also recently been contemplating the possibility that this would be my last year of teaching for a while. After only two full years of teaching and the start of a third, I was tired. I loved my students and I knew many of them cared for me, but I was having doubts. I was going home too exhausted to spend any quality time with my wife and kids. I have since learned that this is not uncommon among new teachers, and that it is a point where many good teachers decide to leave the profession.

During my student teaching I was blessed with a supervising teacher who was a seasoned, confident professional. She encouraged me to use my creativity and to try my own ideas. I enjoyed some success at engaging students through a variety of unconventional activities, usually involving writing. What I learned from her, and what I learned from my first semester as a student teacher, is that teachers who are asked to be creative and, more important, are supported when they are, have extraordinary results.

My next three years of teaching would be an exasperatingly different experience. Although I continued to engage my students toward impressive results, I was doing so in an environment where creativity was suspect, tradition was principal, and new ideas earned only silence, exile, and an abundance of cold stares from one's fellow professionals. I found myself questioning my commitment to what I had hoped would be an enlightening profession. At times, when I would walk into the faculty lounge and the conversations would halt, the occasional snicker lingering in the silence, I felt naked, denuded of any fellowship, and very alone.

Moving On

The following summer I did relocate, following a former professor of mine to northern Georgia. I was contemplating leaving the profession to seek a graduate degree, but with children to raise and bills to pay, I submitted my application to two of the local high schools, resolute that I would teach only at a school that wanted what I had to offer. Both schools contacted me, and during my interviews I expressed my desire to try a variety of new approaches that would engage the students, approaches that tended to break from tradition, but that would get results. The first school I interviewed with never called me back. The second school, after two intense, lengthy, and intimidating interviews, offered me the eleventh-grade AP composition program and Newspaper Journalism.

I accepted the job with excitement and some very high expectations, and decided immediately that this was the opportune time to attempt my novel project. In preparation I began to consider any and all objections that might arise, whether from students, parents, or the administration. I made a list of possible objectives and reasons for wanting my students to write novels as a group. My list grew quickly, and aside from a few ego-related end points, I was impressed with the number of solid objectives I had come up with. Having worked cooperatively on a couple of novels over the previous summer, I knew that the big surprise to the kids wouldn't be the writing, but instead the amount of critical reading they would need to do in order to keep the plot line consistent. If they were set in groups of three as I intended, then they would need to read what had occurred since they had last written on their turn.

Some of the finer points on my list were a realization of the differences in individual writing styles, a need for students to model and adapt their own prose styles, and, hopefully, learning a variety of rhetorical and creative writing techniques that would be incorporated into personal writing styles. A big plus would be the cooperation needed to complete such a project, and I intended to place the responsibilities on the groups to ride each other and insist on quality and deadlines. All in all, the more I thought about it, the more I felt confident that the abundance of merits would support such a project if it were ever brought into question. I made the decision, and all that was left was the implementation.

Novel Expectations

"In this class you will be required to complete an ongoing project that begins today and continues for the entire school year. This assignment will be done out of class and will be due in full during the first week of May. You are going to write novels." I paused and looked up. There was a mixture of astonishment, disbelief, hostility, and excitement in their faces.

I continued. "It is my hope that by writing and working cooperatively on an extensive piece of fiction, you will really begin to understand the distinctiveness of voice, style, and characterization, and that you will learn a handful of rhetorical tools that will enhance the quality of your own writing style. I also expect that you will become a much more critical reader, with a better understanding of your own analytical processes. And lastly, you will become part of a group who completes a manuscript that will be submitted for publication. If nothing else, you get a chance at immortality."

I handed out the assignment, in which I laid out a copious set of rules for the groups to follow, and a handout that would break down the assignment and spell out the details. Handout 5.1 is the list of original rules I gave out the first time I tried the "novel experience." They have since been revised, and the full revision is included with the handouts at the end of this chapter.

And so it began.

After the initial shock, there was some excitement. I talked to the class about plot and character. There were questions, many students wanting to know how

DOUT   **5.1**

The Rules

- Each writing group will have one ongoing novel that must be rotated consistently in the original order that was agreed upon.
- When it is your turn in the rotation (meaning you have just been given "the book"), you will have no more than six (6) days to write no less than six (6) pages. You may write more if you wish (no limit), and you may pass the book earlier than the six days if you wish (as long as your page requirement has been satisfied). If the sixth day falls on a Saturday or Sunday, the novel may be held until the Monday after. **Extended holidays and vacation weekends will be managed by the group leaders—passing will still take place.** When you have written and are ready to pass the disk, log your dates and page counts on the log provided and pass the disk to the next person in your rotation. I recommend you keep a backup of your work in the event of crisis.
- When it is your turn to write on the novel, you may take (write) the book in whatever direction you like. Consistency of writing is recommended, so matching styles (and occasionally tone) will be to your advantage. You may write wherever you like, even if it includes jumping into the middle of a sentence, but you may not revise a group member's writing. **Never delete or erase another writer's work.**
- All novels must be written on a computer (using a word-processing program) and must be kept on the disks that are provided. All group members will decide on what format to save the novels in, and will attempt to save them consistently. Font size should be no larger than 12. **It is strongly recommended you keep a backup file of your disk in the event of disaster.**

---

much they'd get paid if their novel were accepted for publication. We talked about various genres, and I allowed them the freedom to choose, as a group, the genre in which they would write. I gave them what was left of the period to discuss their ideas, and then I gave them the agreement for creative projects (Figure 5.1).

I explained the need for them to discuss the content limits of what they would write, noting that all parent wishes should be respected. Since most of my groups were heterogeneous, I brought up the fact that they should consider what it was each of them as individuals least wanted to see in writing during this project. One very wise group of young ladies teamed up against a boy who was sharing their project. The girls effectively shut down what they feared would come from him. In their agreement they wrote:

> We do not want any farting, any nose picking, no sex (unless discussed ahead of time and approved by each group member), no profanity ('f' word, 'gd', or 's' word), no descriptive nudity, no pornography, and no unexpected violence (unless approved on by group).

FIGURE 5.1   Agreement for the Creative Project

AGREEMENT FOR THE CREATIVE PROJECT

WHAT IS YOUR GROUP NUMBER? _____   **WHAT IS THE DATE?**
_____

PROVIDE YOUR NAMES IN THE ORDER THAT YOU WILL ROTATE YOUR NOVEL:

1st _____   **2nd** _____   **3rd** _____   **4th** _____

IN WHAT FORMAT WILL YOU BE SAVING YOUR WORK: _____

IN THE SPACE PROVIDED BELOW PLEASE WRITE OUT A CLEAR AND SPECIFIC CONTENT AGREEMENT FOR YOUR PROJECT. THIS SHOULD INCLUDE ANYTHING THAT YOU, AS A GROUP, HAVE DEEMED OFFENSIVE AND DO NOT WISH TO SEE WRITTEN. (Please keep your parent's wishes on what you should not read or write in mind here.)

AS A MEMBER OF THIS WRITING GROUP, I AGREE TO RESPECT AND HONOR THIS CONTENT AGREEMENT.

_____   _____   _____   _____

AS A MEMBER OF THIS WRITING GROUP, I AGREE THAT THIS ASSIGNMENT IS A COOPERATIVE ENDEAVOR, AND AT NO TIME WILL I CLAIM IT, OR ANY PART OF IT, AS MY OWN.

_____   _____   _____   _____

HONOR STATEMENT:

I have read the instructions and rules for this cooperative project and have asked all the questions that come to mind at this time. At all times I will honor my obligations as a group member and act with integrity in all aspects of the assignment. On this I give my word.

Printed name_____   Signature_____

Printed name_____   Signature_____

Printed name_____   Signature_____

Printed name_____   Signature_____

Rob, the young man who was being ganged up on, protested loudly, declaring that they had taken all the fun out of this assignment already, but in the end he signed the agreement. Another group, anticipating something I had not foreseen, wrote:

> There will be no using the Lord's name in vain.
> There will be no teasing vegetarians.
> There will be no satanic sacrifices.

One group I had put together as an experiment because of their widely diverse skill levels, but awesome creativity, addressed the content agreement with a much more open mind:

> We are leaving all avenues open. If, however, any questionable content arises, it will be modified at the group's discretion. If, at any point, any member objects to any word, subject, or situation within this work, it will be discussed until all parties are satisfied.

The excitement in the room was contagious, and I walked around the room noting that the students were taking the assignment seriously. With a few minutes left in class, I halted them and told them that I wanted them to read and sign the "Honor Statement" portion of the agreement. I discussed the need for them to create an honor system within their group so that no one was taking advantage of anyone else. Since all passing of the novel would take place within the group, they would need to select a group leader to monitor the rotation, document page counts, and keep track of the passing of days. I was pleased and felt confident that they understood exactly what it was that I was expecting. It took me a month or so to realize that I should have been a little more worried.

Formatting

Because the novel was to be written entirely out of class, I had suggested specific individuals as group leaders, based on reliability and talent. I wanted contacts whom I could talk with at any point to get some straight answers. The first problems that I encountered were the students who had no concept of how to save a file to disk. Many of these were the group leaders, and they were mystified when their work wound up in some weird file on their hard drive. Sometimes the person receiving the disk would try to open the file, only to find that no writing had taken place. Many of the students had no concept of file compatibility and had completely ignored (or been ignorant of) the initial format agreement.

For example, one student would save the file in MS Word, and the next would try to open it in Works. Many of these students, I realized, had become accustomed to blaming their computers for delays and were delighted with an assignment that allowed them the freedom to continue the practice unabated.

With so many excuses coming from so many students, it was impossible for me to determine who was lying and who had valid problems. Almost all of the problems in the initial stages were related to how students were saving their work (and where they were saving it), so I suspended our class work and opted for a one-day workshop on saving files. To be honest, I viewed the ensuing "technology workshop" as a decent opportunity to intensify the technological expectations for the assignment, and it seemed reasonable that the students sooner or later would have to learn the intricacies of properly formatting a disk.

I decided that the formatting differences could be addressed by having everyone save their files in a "rich text" (RTF) format or a "text" (TXT) format. I had students gather around my ancient 486, non-Pentium computer and demonstrated the procedures for saving a file to disk and for changing the format of a file during the save. I had the more computer-savvy students group up with the computer-illiterate students and explain the process to them. To expedite the process, some students even created a set of written instructions for their fellow group members. Although I looked forward to seeing the project get underway, I still had a few unexpected wrinkles to iron out.

Honor

The next two weeks, I checked the logs, opened the files to verify page counts, and was happy to see that the novels were actually progressing. It was Sarah, one of my group leaders, who came to me before class one day and opened my eyes to how blatantly I was being deceived by many of my honor-bound AP students. She was worried, and rightfully so, because she knew that it would only be a matter of time until I began inspecting the novels more closely, and would discover that there were some serious problems. Sarah was obviously uncomfortable, and she was reluctant to give me names or specifics, but she told me that I might want to examine the disks more carefully at the next due date. That day I called in all the disks, and could tell immediately by the side looks and raised eyebrows that something was wrong.

When I set up the novel experience, I did so with the understanding that I would not be able to read each group's entire novel as it progressed. I did plan on reading bits and pieces, but I was being realistic in what I knew I could do and what I couldn't. I was at a point now, though, where I needed to find out what it was that had caused Sarah to come to me so covertly. After school the following day, I began going through each of the novels. Most of the groups were up to approximately forty pages of text. As I skimmed their words, I began to understand the cause of Sarah's alarm. With each novel I scanned, I came across a variety of similar problems. What became apparent is that a few students had been talking and sharing specific techniques to cheat the page count, and they had been doing so rather excessively. Page breaks were inserted randomly. Text from previous pages had been copied and pasted several times over on several different pages. On one novel, I found a complete, seven-page history paper that had been pasted into the novel with no attempt at continuity or transitions. I printed out that section and took it to the history department. Sure enough, it was an assignment that had been turned in weeks before. I was upset. These were good students who had signed an oath of honor. I doubted my ninth graders from the previous year would have ever tried anything so blatant or deceptive. They simply would not have done the assignment, and then apologized. This was worse. These students were spending time and energy to take credit for something they weren't doing.

I knew that I could narrow the downfall of my novel project to a few students if I tried, but the problem was that I didn't want to punish anyone unfairly. I did have quite a few good, hardworking students. The next day I halted my schedule and called all of the group leaders into the hall. I pointed out that I had come across some questionable problems on most of the disks. Two groups out of ten were doing a fabulous job and had no problems, but all of the others had some serious problems that needed immediate addressing. I informed them that, as group leaders, they were responsible for monitoring their groups, and for informing me of any member not honoring their agreement.

I handed back the disks, informed them that I would recheck them in one day, and that if any disk contained *any* page breaks, their group would receive a failing grade. I informed them that if any disk contained *any* text that was repetitive, their group would receive a failing grade. I informed them that if any of the disks contained *any* text that was even slightly suspect of not being original and written specifically for the novel, their group would receive a failing grade. I also informed them that from this point forward, all disks were to be handed to me for counts, and that I would back them up, check them, and log in appropriate days and counts myself. One last requirement I made was that I now wanted word counts instead of page counts. I would require 1,700 words of writing instead of six pages for each turn. Some of the group leaders were honestly confused, but I could see the embarrassment in others. I knew most of them had been aware of what their group had been doing.

Once we were back in class, I informed the class of the new changes. I pointed out that once the disks were handed to me on the following day, it was possible I would be removing several students from this project for cheating. I did not point the finger or ask that it be pointed, but I did make myself clear that if the new word count did not closely match what it should have, based on the page count that had previously been turned in, I would need to make some adjustments. I informed them that any member of a group who failed to do the assigned work during the allotted time would be removed permanently from a group, and that they would have to do the entire project on their own if they wished to pass the class. The last point I made to both my AP classes was that if at any time I found anything suspect on a disk, I would go first to the group leader for an explanation. If, at that point, I felt there was a problem that the leader should have brought to my attention and did not, I would fail them for the project, at least in the current grading period. In front of the class, I asked all of the group leaders if any of them wished to be replaced. None did.

AP students are an interesting breed. They stared at me, wounded and incredulous, but also with a sense of shame. The next day all of the disks were turned in, and all of them contained word counts that I found acceptable. I had heard through the grapevine that, after my lecture, there had been a panicked scramble that lasted late into the night where students set up times and places to pass the novels and share in righting the wrong they had perpetuated. This late-night flurry of writing was the turning point in the project. Students who were accustomed to getting away with occasional deceptions were now faced with the reality of the year-long assignment. The group leaders' penchant for good grades would ensure an end to further discrepancies. The group leaders began communicating with me on a regular basis, informing me of those who had gone beyond their allotted time and those whose writing did not seem to fit—work that in most cases was the result of someone writing without reading what had been written in advance. The conscientiousness of the group leaders made it easy to address individuals personally, and their diligence also reinforced the need for members of the group to read carefully and to take their contributions seriously.

Of the ten groups, one was having difficulties. The group leader, Lauren, came to me one day after school to let me know that she had covered for one of her group members on more than one occasion when he made excuses of being too busy. She was worried because he was asking her again, and she did not have the time to do his share of writing as well as her own. I thanked her for coming to me and confronted the boy the next day. He made an abundance of excuses and insisted that Lauren had offered to do the writing for him. He was already doing poorly in my class, seldom did the reading assignments, and rarely turned in any homework. His lack of reliability left me few options. I removed him from the group and informed him that he would be required to do the assignment on his own if he wished to pass the class. With Lauren's group down to two students, I watched them closely, and even occasionally took a turn for the absent member. Soon, I became dismayed when the other girl in the group began failing to turn in the disk on the required days. When Lauren or I would ask for the disk, she would turn it in, late, often without having written a word. I was left no choice but to remove her from the group as well.

This left me with few options for Lauren. She was alone, and I didn't feel that it would be fair to her to have to write the whole novel herself, given the fact that she had done her share and more. When I asked her if she would like to scrap her book and join another group, she queried me as to whether I could find any volunteers in my journalism class to work with her. My copy editor was famous at our school as a writer, and when I asked him about the novel project, he willingly jumped at the chance. I knew him to be extremely reliable. I was impressed with Lauren for not wanting to give up her book. A day or so after the young man joined Lauren's group, I received a transfer student from out of state. Lauren's group had bounced back to three. The two students who had been taken out of Lauren's group did not attempt to do the assignment on their own (nor did they end up passing my class). However, the word went out to those students who had been on the fringe—those who had been turning in their disks late or who were not fulfilling their full word counts—that I meant business. As a result, I saw a dramatic increase in student motivation.

Virus

Around the third month of the project, we encountered a computer virus that promised to wipe out much of the students' hard work. One smart, technologically astute student brought me his disk one morning and informed me that it had crashed his computer. Within the next few days, I had all of the disks, and almost everyone had complained of a similar experience. Although I had developed a standing rule that computer problems in this class were not an acceptable excuse, I had what appeared to be a genuine epidemic on my hands.

Up until this point, I had been enjoying a great deal of parental support for the novel project. When computers began crashing, however, I began receiving phone calls. It seemed that my computer at school, the computer I used to read word counts and back up the files, had contracted a nasty little Stealth virus. While I was opening the files and backing up the disks, I was also passing on the virus to my students, who, in turn, were taking them home and infecting their own computers. The Stealth virus wasn't always a fatal virus to computers, but in the case of my classes, it seemed to be wreaking havoc. I went immediately to the local computer retailer and purchased one of the latest antivirus programs. I created emergency boot disks for the students to take home and began scanning each disk before backing it up. Eventually the virus was destroyed and students regained control over their novels.

Editors

As we neared the end of the school year and the novel word counts began to reach into the seventy and eighty thousands, the student's motivation seemed to increase. The AP test was upon us, and I decided to use most of the remaining class time after the test for revision and editing of the novels. I announced a due date two weeks in advance and checked out the computer lab so that groups could divide the work. Every student would have access to a computer so that they could revise during class.

During the days before the novels were due, I became enthralled at the levels of stress that the students were reaching over their books. Frantic emails appeared in my inbox, and students called my house late at night, complaining that their computers had turned evil again and were hiding revised files. Those who were wise and had begun printing out small sections all along the way were finding that their printers had never been asked to print anything so lengthy. Pages mysteriously disappeared and ink cartridges dried up. Even though many students had valid problems, I held firm, and calmly told them that I didn't want any excuses. I wanted novels.

On the due date, students handed in ten lengthy rough drafts. All groups had finished. Prior to the due date, I had selected ten of my best readers from the classes to participate in the editing and analysis of the novels. These students were given an editor number, a different color highlighter, and one of the novels. Their job was to read the novel, highlighting and commenting on places that needed revision. The editors were to give a one-page, typed analysis of the novel and its problems to each group. The editors then gave me the novels and their analysis, and I gave them a new novel. Each novel was read and edited by two different editors.

With three weeks of school left, I decided to save the last week for final revisions and preparations for submission, so I could give each editor only one week per novel. Despite the brief timeline, the editors seemed to enjoy the experience, and did more than I had expected by way of commenting and suggesting improvements.

When the groups received the novels back for the final revision, they were stunned by all the comments and editing. Lauren's group had turned in a novel that contained 180 pages. After heeding the comments and eliminating the first chapter entirely, they finished with a book of 120 pages—a small novella. Many of the books had finished with flaws that the editors had pointed out. One group had forgotten that they had killed a character in one scene and had him reappearing on several instances throughout the rest of the book. Editor comments made a vast improvement in the quality of revision, and most students took their peers' close readings and criticisms to heart.

With only a few days left, I brought in my *Writer's Digest* market book, and the groups began looking for book publishing companies. The students were surprised to find that many book publishers only wanted books that were submitted from agents. A large portion of the market simply requested a synopsis and a sample chapter. Most of the groups wanted to send their entire manuscript, and narrowed their search to the few companies that requested full manuscripts. Some of the groups prepared the requested sample chapters and began writing their cover letters.

On the last day of regular classes all groups had finished their novels. I had requested that students take them to the local copy store and have them bound with covers, but once again, the students surprised me with the level of their creativity. The covers were creative and colorful. One by one, the groups stood in front of the class, held their novel for all to see, and announced, "We wrote a novel!" It was an exciting moment for the students, who broke into spontaneous applause and animated discussions afterwards. Obviously, they were proud of what they had done, and I was proud of them as well.

Critical Reading

Looking back on the first year, I was able to gauge what had been good about the assignment and what had not. I knew that I would make changes for the following year. One of the realities that I am still addressing about "Novel Expectations" is that often the students will not completely read what was written between turns before they write. The inability of students to read critically is perhaps the single most frustrating aspect of the project. With my current students, I had the benefit of my reputation for meaning business, and have not had to deal with any attempts at deception or cheating. I have not had to remove any students from the project since that first year. If asked what it was that surprised me the most about the novel project during the first year, I'd have to say the quality of editing and revision I saw by the end of the experience. When students finally complete the novel, they gain a sense of ownership and professionalism that is all too rare among adolescents.

On request, I donated copies of all the novels to the media center, and our school librarians created a "student-written novels" section, something the administration has become very proud of. One of the media specialists was a little taken aback by the language used in several of the books, but I believe she appreciated the freedom the students were given and the maturity they showed with that freedom. To date, none of the novels has been accepted for publication, though many of the students who were part of this experience have gone on to publish several times in magazines and books. Recently I received a call from Natalie, one of the group leaders from the first "novel" class. She had been accepted for publication in the latest *Chicken Soup for the Soul* book. Additionally, her group had been asked to add thirty thousand words to their novel manuscript and resubmit. They are working on it still, on their own, without a due date or grade attached. In the first year of "Novel Expectations," nineteen of twenty-one students who chose to take AP Language and Composition passed.

Handouts

Figures 5.2 and 5.3 are the most current handouts that I use for the project. The "Rules" handout is quite comprehensive, and the log sheet is still a very effective means of monitoring word counts and days of possession.

Sequence of Activities

Three days at the beginning of the semester are needed to set up "Novel Expectations." From there, the project becomes primarily an out-of-class experience that requires weekly checks, occasional workshops, and student/group conferences.

FIGURE 5.2   Rules for Novel Unit

RULES FOR NOVEL EXPECTATIONS— A COOPERATIVE PROJECT

You, as a group, are going to write a novel. This assignment will be an out of class, ongoing project for most of the school year and will be due in full during the first week of May, _____.

HERE'S WHY:
- By writing and working cooperatively on an extensive piece of fiction, you, as an individual, will gain a deep understanding of the difference in author styles and techniques.
- You will learn various formatting options for word processing programs.
- Your writing skills will increase and mature.
- You will become a more critical reader.
- You will be part of a finished manuscript that your group will submit for publication.

THE RULES:
- Each writing group will have one on-going novel that must be rotated consistently in the original order that was agreed upon.
- When it is your turn in the rotation (meaning you have just been given "the book"), you will have no more than seven (7) days to write no less than 1850 words. You may write more than this amount if you wish (no limit), and you may pass the book earlier than the seven days if you wish (as long as your word requirement has been satisfied). If the seventh day falls on Saturday, the novel must be passed on the Friday before. If the seventh day falls on Sunday, the novel may be held until the Monday after. **The group leaders and I will manage extended holidays and vacation weekends—passing will still take place—occasionally via email.** When you have written and are ready to pass the disk, simply hand it to me in class, and you are done. I will check for viruses, log the word count, back up the file, and pass the disk on to the next person.
- When it is your turn to write on the novel, you may take (write) the book in whatever direction you like. Consistency of writing is recommended, so matching styles (and occasionally tone) will be to your advantage. You may write wherever you like, even if it includes jumping into the middle of a sentence, but you may not revise a group member's writing. **Never delete or erase another writer's work.**
- All novels must be written on a computer (or word processor), and must be kept on the disks that are provided. **NOTHING ELSE IS ALLOWED ON THIS DISK!** All novels will be saved in either *rich text* (RTF) format, or *text* (TXT)—this is mandatory for sharing purposes. Font size should be either 10 or 12 (Times New Roman or Arial), single spaced, and one inch margins all around (we will double space them after deadline). **It is strongly recommended you keep a back-up file of your disk in the event of disaster.** If you do not have a computer, mine is available on a prearranged basis. Also, libraries and friends are a good resource for access to the technology needed.

CONTENT MATTERS:
     I do not believe in censuring good writing. Pornography is not good writing, nor is profanity just for the sake of writing profanity. Since this is a "writing assignment," and what you write could offend the others in your writing groups, I will require you, as a group, to define your boundaries of what is offensive to you and what is not—**in writing to each other.**

ABOUT HONOR:
     You are expected to be on your honor for this assignment and to treat the members of your writing group with respect and courtesy. Please do not ask anybody to cover for you, lie for you, or to do your work—that is not how people of integrity behave. The penalty for cheating (to any degree) on this assignment will be removal from a writing group, at which point you will be required to undertake this assignment on your own, thereby tripling the writing requirements for yourself. **Being in a writing group is a privilege that requires working cooperatively.** Cheating is defined as doing (or not doing) anything outside the rules for this assignment.

FIGURE 5.2   **Rules for Novel Unit** (*continued*)

WHAT I EXPECT:
        I expect your group to write a novel. I expect you to contribute your best writing to this project. As we progress in this class, and you learn new techniques and skills, I expect to see them put to use in your writing (for instance—mood and tone through imagery. . .). I expect you to work with your group. I expect you to become a more critical reader and writer. I expect you to use your own ideas and let others use theirs—*NEVER TELL A GROUP MEMBER WHAT YOU WOULD LIKE THEM TO WRITE WHEN IT IS THEIR TURN!!!*

ABOUT PUBLISHING:
        Once you have finished you manuscript and submitted it for publication, there is a chance it will sell. If all group members have lived up to their requirements, there should be no question that the book belongs to all members of the group, and that any royalties should be divided equally. *Note: If you are under 18 and a publishing company shows an interest in your manuscript, parents will need to be involved in the final contract, and any disputes or objections that could arise will more than likely kill that particular contract.*

ABOUT GRADING:
        This project will receive one major grade for each grading period (approximately 10% to 15%). Grading will be subjective on the following criteria. Individual effort and writing quality (based on the word logs and written work), and group participation (doing your share and then some). Also, I will consult with each of you from time to time, as well as your group leader, and hopefully receive some insight into your experience and learning process.

HOUSEKEEPING MATTERS:
   • If you do not reach your required word length on your turn, points will be deducted from your grade.
   • If you fail to pass the novel within the time allotted, points will be deducted from your grade.
   • If at anytime you violate your group's content agreement, you run the risk of being removed from your group—at which time you will be required to fulfill the requirements for this assignment on your own.
   • If a disk gets lost or destroyed, and there is no back-up, you will fail this assignment—**make sure someone in your group is keeping a back-up!** I will also back the disk up, but this is a courtesy and having a back-up is your responsibility.

FINAL NOTE:
 Because of the nature of this assignment, it will be necessary for me to appoint group leaders to monitor the progress and quality of your novels. These individuals will have the added responsibility of informing me of any problems your group may be having, informing your group when a member is past their deadline, and seeing that all work is done to specified requirements, and that it is turned in on time. I would also recommend these individuals keep a back-up disk of all work completed. On the due date, your group will have a finished novel of approximately 200 pages to present to me. I will then assign critical readers (and editors) to critique your novel and make suggestions. From there, we revise, put it all together, and send it out. Good luck, and if you have any questions or concerns, please ask.

Day 1: Setting the Parameters

1. Hand out the parameters for "Novel Expectations," then go over them slowly (with students following along). Explain the objectives, expectations, and procedures for the year, and answer any questions.
2. Students use whatever time remains to begin discussing possible ideas or characters for the novel.

FIGURE 5.3   Cooperative Project Writing Log

COOPERATIVE PROJECT WRITING LOG

This log is kept by me, and will be maintained to determine both individual and group grades for this project.

Person passing book	Date passed	Total days held	Finishing word count	Total words written	Book passed to / date

Day 2: Signing the Agreements

1. Give students honor statements and content agreements for signatures.
2. Groups begin discussing plot lines, conflicts, possible characters, and settings for their novels.

Day 3: Setting and Plot

1. Give students half the class to complete a tentative plot summary, describe the setting, and write down ideas for characters.
2. Discuss formatting options for floppy disks. Show students how to save a file to "text" format as well as "rich text."

Samples from the novel *Wine*
by Lauren Parker and Rob Jones

Page 22

The mayor smiled with a sly grin and thoughts of how this could actually help him get re-elected. The poor man who lost his son, but stayed strong throughout it all, why not vote for him?

"How does that sound to you?" Jake blew cigarette smoke into the musty air of the office.

"Sounds fine to me," he said with a smirk on his face. "Call me if you need any help."

"I will. Don't worry. They don't usually get away from me." And Jake smiled.

The passing train summoned up huge clouds of dust, which crashed over it like waves on either side, until breaking in the dirty rail yard. Thomas and James ducked low to avoid the billowing dirt and steam thrown off by the train, as well as the watchful eyes of the yard bosses. When he'd located the right car and was quite sure no one was looking, Thomas dashed for an open flat car, swung one leg over the side, and toppled in, signaling James to follow. Tossing their meager bags into one corner, they ducked low as the train pulled out, slow at first, then howling through the countryside on its way to Chicago. They both relaxed in the car as the land slid by.

"So who was he?" said Thomas. "Why'd you hit him?"

"He was . . ." James faltered. "He was a friend. I was just mad, I suppose. I just swung—didn't think about it. Next thing I know, he's down, bleedin', just staring up at the ceiling."

It's not your fault, then. Too bad." It struck James as funny, those words: too bad. Yes, it was too bad, he thought. Too bad for him, too bad for his father, too bad for everyone. The wind whipped at his hair, and he smelled a dairy as the train shot through a tiny farming town. Just for a moment, he thought he smelled death. He saw that face staring up at him, covered in a fine mist of blood, eyes blank and accusing. It wasn't my fault, James tried to convince himself. But the air grew stale and rotten around them, as if telling James what it thought. He rolled over and waited for Chicago to arrive.

From page 66

After a moment, she sat up, painfully, and sipped at the water glass on the bedside table. Her husband's form lay beneath the striped sheets, youthful and thin despite a slight middle-age bulge at the waist. Sleeping. Calm. Like the rest of the little town. She caught herself just before she flung the glass at the armoire mirror, and placed it gently back on the bedside table. Mustn't lose composure. Composure, composure. To hell with composure! She almost screamed, wanted to slap her husband for being able to sleep, wanted to set the town afire for laying [sic] in their beds while her son was out there alone, lost, dead. They could not know, with their little troubles and petty thoughts. She hadn't even known. His face appeared again, there in the dark, and she could almost feel him under her fingertips, like a shadow in the room. She felt the bed under her, felt the silence pounding in the room, and felt the emptiness inside her. She hadn't even known. Her arms fell to her side, and she collapsed, exhausted, into the wide soft bed. She had lost her world. And hadn't known it until he was gone.

Sample from the Novel *A Day in a Life*
by Travis Canova, Komal Patel, and Drew Neslin

Chapter 39, pages 160–161

The next morning I awoke. I opened my eyes. Sweetie was nowhere to be seen. Where had she gone to? I decided to go look for her. I looked towards the lake; she wasn't there. I walked down the hill and into the field; she wasn't there. I looked by the creek where we first met; she wasn't there. I looked in our village; she wasn't there.

I walked up the dusty trail towards the giant mountains where I had spent the last year of my young, unfulfilled life. I kept walking and walking. I climbed upward. The sun was bright and unbearable. I began to sweat. I decided to search for the place that had so much promise. Some place beautiful and peaceful. I kept traversing upwards. After awhile, I approached two gates. Two gates I had never seen before. One side was beautiful. The other was dark and treacherous. I turned around and looked towards the place I had come. I saw nothing. I had nowhere to go but in. I decided the gate on the left was more appealing. I saw some of my family. I pulled the handle down. It was locked. The sun was laughing. I tried the gate on the right. It opened with ease. The darkness frowned on me.

"Wait a minute!" I remembered the key I found in the village of the Kruntuk Indians. It was the only thing I kept. It was mysterious and I knew it must have been good for something so I kept it. "Hell yes!" I went to fit the key into its hole. One problem. It did not fit. It did not fit. My smile quickly turned to a frown. I looked back towards where I had come from. There was nothing. I had to enter the door on the right.

So I entered cautiously. Tears flooded my eyes. The steep mountain that seemed to rise for eternity was the only thing that lay ahead once I was in. I turned around and tried to leave the entrance. It was now locked. Bridge and Sweetie were probably around here somewhere. I was stuck inside with the never-ending mountain ahead.

Eternity?

OUTCOMES

1. Students learned how to write a novel.

2. Students learned how to write collaboratively.

3. Students learned to use language effectively.

4. Students learned the importance of style, tone, and consistency of voice.

5. Students learned the fundamentals of getting a novel published.

6. I realized that not all students are completely honest and hard-working.

7. I learned how to prevent loopholes in the novel project.

8. I learned how to systemically battle computer viruses.

9. Students learned to use a word-processing program across platforms.

ACTIVITIES

1. Place students in writing groups.

2. Lay out the rules and expectations for writing a novel.

3. Make sure students understand the expectations. Have students sign an honor pledge and content agreement.

4. Students discuss plot, characters, setting, and style.

5. Demonstrate to students how to save files, prevent viruses, and back up files.

6. Identify and work with group leaders.

7. Monitor student progress regularly.

8. Select editors.

9. Have editors write one-page analysis of a novel and its problems.

10. Hand back novels with editors' comments.

11. Discuss novels and revision.

12. Students work on revisions.

13. Students select book publisher to whom to submit their work.

14. Students bind novels and create covers.

15. Students read from their novels and celebrate the deed.

16. Students send their manuscripts to publishers.

6 The Conduct of Life

Teaching philosophy and rhetoric
with an edge

TIME: Four to five weeks

To Build a Fire

I was talking with two football players, George and Jacob.

I asked, "What do you like to read?"

Both admitted that they never voluntarily read anything other than the sports page of the local newspaper.

Then I asked them, "What are you going to do upon graduation?"

George shifted uneasily, "Get a scholarship and play football." Jacob nodded in agreement.

It was March, well past the date most college prospects sign the letter of intent and neither had received so much as a postcard from a football coach of a university or junior college.

"If you don't get a scholarship, what will you do?" I asked.

"Maybe go to college somewhere," said George.

"Where have you applied?" I asked.

"Haven't got around to that yet, but I will. I mean, I'll start applying if it turns out I don't get a ride. But, I'd rather go for free."

It was obvious that neither had seriously considered the possibility that they might not get a scholarship, even at this late date. Heck, they had yet to even contact a college for an application. Needless to say, they would not even get a look at institutions that required a high school grade-point average of B or higher, such as Tennessee, Texas Tech, Washington, Wisconsin, Florida State, Illinois, and Nebraska, or any of the familiar "football schools." In fact, March was beyond the required admissions application deadline of most colleges and universities in the area.

"I can't go to college if I don't get a scholarship," said Jacob. "Can't afford it."

I looked over at George and asked, "If you went to college, do you have any idea what you might want to major in?"

"I don't know. Maybe business or accounting; something easy. It's got to be a job where I don't have to read or write much, where I can take off when I want to, not work very hard, but still get paid a lot of money. I hate to read, but writing's the worst."

Jacob thought a few more seconds and said, "If I don't get a scholarship, I'll probably get a job. Something where I make a lot of money."

"Both of you seem to want a lot of money," I said. "But someone has to want to pay you for doing something. What can you do?"

Jacob shrugged.

"Well, Jacob, what do you like to do?"

Jacob looked out the window and grimaced. "Play football."

"Surely there's something else that's okay to do. Do you like to eat?"

"Yeah, I like to eat and play football." Jacob laughed.

George nodded and broke into a wide grin. Then, suddenly an inspiration came to him—"Oh, and I like to fish."

I felt like saying, "George and Jacob, you think employers are going to line up for the opportunity to pay you to ride around in a boat and fish?" but I didn't. Instead, I tried to get them to think about what they liked to do, what they disliked, and what they might want to do with their lives, at least in the short term. Here they sat, two hulking eighteen-year-olds, uncomfortable in their molded plastic and metal desks, complacent in their preposterous beliefs of scholarships, scraping by in senior English, with no clue of what to do in a few months when the state would no longer require that they show up for first period.

Emerson wrote, "We refuse sympathy and intimacy with people, as if we waited for some better sympathy and intimacy to come. But whence and when? Tomorrow will be like today. Life wastes itself whilst we are preparing to live" (Emerson 2000, p. 217). Jacob and George were oblivious to their own talents, had an open dislike for reading and writing, and had no idea about what they were going to do from June until, well, forever. Jacob and George considered school boring and irrelevant. They just didn't understand what school had to do with their lives beyond furnishing them an opportunity to wear the school colors on Friday nights in fall under the stadium lights.

When your day is filled with bureaucratic directives, discipline problems, interruptions, and the normal fluctuations of adolescent hormones, it is understandable to wish Jacob and George were in somebody else's class. They are not the easiest students with whom to work.

In the same class with Jacob and George was a girl named Carlyn, a straight-A honor roll mainstay who was as aloof as she was sardonic. In her way, Carlyn was more difficult to work with than Jacob and George. Although Carlyn had brains, she was petulant and hypercritical. Her usual reaction to assignments was to roll her eyes as if what I had suggested was one of the most inane things she'd ever heard in her life. But she was haughty with her classmates as well.

I'm not against a teacher practicing triage (assigning time to students based upon the urgency of their needs or their chances for success), but when I first started teaching, I would expend great time and effort working with students like

Jacob and George because they obviously needed as much help as they could get. And I would tend to ignore students like Carlyn, who had obvious talent, but who tended to be belligerent. As a teacher, I have learned that you cannot write off anybody. You never know who will blossom, so you have to keep plugging away doing the best you know how. If you make the learning environment fun and stimulating, then students will participate. If you make the learning environment dull and menacing, then they won't.

Rather than brave Carlyn's icy, deep waters, the tack of most teachers (me included) is to forge some kind of unwritten truce with her—don't give me many problems, turn in your assignments on time, and I'll not hassle you. As a result of such implicit agreements, Carlyn probably liked school even less than Jacob and George. She probably cared about old Mr. Baines and English as much as she cared about the lyrics of the national anthem of the Czech Republic (not much). What could Carlyn really do if she gave an assignment her sincere, best effort? I had no idea. All I knew was that she always turned in her work on time, managed to maintain an A average, and was prone to making snide remarks about the relevance of my assignments.

I created the "Conduct of Life" experience with students like Carlyn, Jacob, and George in mind. I wanted to push them out of their complacency into the undiscovered country of their potential. I wanted them to think deeply about what they were doing with their lives and where they wanted to go, beyond next weekend. If I failed, at least the cause seemed worthy.

"Conduct of Life" offers several very different kinds of readings—poems, essays, short stories—and requires students to examine the belief systems of various writers and poets through close reading, inference, and analysis. Once students read, discuss, and scrutinize the philosophies of others, I ask them to write about their own beliefs through poetry, art, essay, or short story. Then I move students from the sometimes abstract nature of philosophic thinking to the more concrete arena of film. Toward this end, students make a short video based upon their essays and stories. Finally, students rewrite their essays and stories, integrating aspects of the video—images, sounds, language, and pacing—into their writing.

"Conduct of Life" is lengthy and complex, requiring some planning, the orchestration of several key discussions, and the acquisition (or borrowing) of books and equipment. Despite the preparation time, students responded to the unit with great enthusiasm, excitement, and a sense of fun. Not only was the quality of student work astounding, the "Conduct of Life" experience engendered full participation and a palpable sense of excitement. Even George said, "It was okay."

Philosophers and writers since before the time of Plato have pondered certain questions: What is love? What do I like? What do I dislike? What is the meaning of life? How should I conduct myself through life? For some of my students, these lessons might well be the last time they would ponder such questions in an academic setting.

In the course of the "Conduct of Life" experience, students read numerous philosophic essays, a short story, some hard-hitting articles depicting ethics in action, and a handful of poems. They wrote a definition of love, listed some aspirations, composed a poem (a pantoum), wrote an essay, produced a video, and completed a fairly lengthy final paper. To give a feel for the progression of student thought and work throughout the sequence, I focus on samples from Carlyn. One week into the unit, on his eighteenth birthday, Jacob withdrew from school. George remained in school and participated in most of the activities, although he was often absent. I had to scramble a little to keep him up-to-date.

Although the class was an eleventh-grade English class, the "Conduct of Life" unit is adaptable for any grade and any track, untracked, remedial, or advanced.

Sequence of Activities

Day 1: The Lowdown on Love

I asked students for some cliches, lyrics, or stories they knew about love. "You know, phrases such as, 'Love makes the world go 'round.'" Students thought for a few seconds, then responded.

"All's fair in love and war."

"What the world needs now is love."

"Love is the drug."

"Love is like oxygen."

"Love burns."

I asked, "Remember that story, *A Tale of Two Cities*? The character Sydney Carton sacrifices his life so that his aristocratic double Charles Darnay can be with Lucie, the love of Sydney's life. What kind of love would that be? Giving up your life so that your girlfriend can be with somebody else."

"Stupid love."

"Anyone do that a fool."

"When you dead, you dead, but you can always find a new girlfriend."

Most students feigned that they didn't remember *Tale of Two Cities*, but they seemed to get the point. Then I asked, "Is love really so powerful? Why are so many contemporary songs about love?"

"What's Love Got to Do with It?"

"Love Don't Cost a Thing."

"Love Will Never Do."

"Almost every song is about love, sir."

The conversation about love seemed to stir them up. "Are contemporary songs really about love or they more about crushes? What is the difference between a crush—infatuation—and love?" Students had many answers.

"Infatuation lasts about a day; love lasts a week or more."

"Infatuation is mostly about sex, you know, biology. Love is about a relationship, getting to know someone as a person."

"When you got a crush on someone, you think they can do no wrong. But then you get to know them and the crush ends."

The class laughed and I managed a smile.

Then I asked, "Can love be enduring, or is it by nature ephemeral?"

"My mom and dad have been married for forever. Love's enduring."

"If you find the right person, love can last, but it's hard to find that person."

"It's only natural that excitement wears off over time. Like when you first go on the roller coaster, you're kind of scared and pumped up. After you've ridden it twenty times, it's still fun, but the rush just isn't there anymore."

I looked around the room. Every person in class, even Carlyn, Jacob, and George, seemed to be attentive. I was quiet for a few seconds, then closed my eyes and said, "Love is a fire. It burns, hurts, transforms." I let the words trickle out of my mouth slowly, doing my darnedest to imitate the commanding voice of former British actor Richard Burton (and not pulling it off very well). "Leonard Cohen says that love is 'the world's excuse for being ugly.'"

When I opened my eyes again, I looked around the room. Several of the girls sighed heavily.

"Oooh, my gosh! How depressing. Baines, you're one sick puppy."

George was smiling, "Cool."

"Is love a fire?"

George said, "You know, sometimes love burn you up, leave you all scarred up."

I looked at Jacob. "He right, Jacob?"

Jacob said, "Man's crazy. I don't know."

It had been the most response that I had gotten out of George all year. Then, I handed Carlyn a copy of Shakespeare's Sonnet 116 ("Let me not to the marriage of true minds . . . ") and said quietly, "I'm going to ask you to read this aloud in class. Look it over, okay? Read slowly, make it dramatic."

Carlyn rolled her eyes and sighed, but she looked it over. Meanwhile, I tried to stir up the class about the many potentialities of love. Although the class conversation was heating up nicely, I interrupted at an opportune moment and asked Carlyn to read. I said, "Here's a view quite in opposition to love as a fire."

Carlyn read deliberately, but without much emotion.

"Let's hear it again," George asked.

Carlyn read it a second time, this time, even more slowly. After Carlyn's second rendition, the class was quiet. "So, does love burn you or redeem you? Carlyn, what about it?"

Carlyn looked uncomfortable, a nice change. "Neither, really," she said. I let the silence hang in the air and continued to look at her. "What?" she said, "What do you want me to say?"

"Only what you think, Carlyn."

"I don't know what I think. I've never been in love, so I have no idea if love's a fire or this sickening lovey-dovey thing that turns your mind to mush."

"It's fire, dude," said George.

"Is that the metaphor you would use to describe your conception of love, George—fire?"

"Yeah, man, I guess so."

"That's awful."

HANDOUT 6.1

Sonnet 116 by William Shakespeare

Let me not to the marriage of true minds
Admit impediments. Love is not love
Which alters when it alteration finds,
Or bends with the remover to remove.
O no, it is an ever-fixèd mark
That looks on tempests and is never shaken;
It is the star to every wand'ring bark,
Whose worth's unknown, although his height be taken.
Love's not time's fool, though rosy lips and cheeks
Within his bending sickle's compass come.
Love alters not with his brief hours and weeks,
But bears it out ev'n to the edge of doom.
If this be error and upon me proved,
I never writ, nor no man ever loved.

"Love is beautiful, like a flower. But, if you don't treat it right, it'll die."

I said, "There's a song by Neil Young called 'Love is a Rose.' He says that love is beautiful, but if you try to hold it, all you're going to get is a handful of thorns."

I had brought a ton of handouts with me, but wasn't sure which ones I'd use, if any of them. I wanted to see what students had to say about love first, then I'd select the reading. Because most students did not dispute that love had thorns or might be like fire, I chose an essay by Emerson, "The Conduct of Life," which offered an optimistic, hopeful view. I said, "I want you to pay close attention to Emerson's perspectives on life, love, and happiness. What is Emerson's philosophy of life? I want you to write down two passages from the essay that you feel most accurately express Emerson's views on life, love, and happiness." On the chalkboard, I wrote, "Write two passages from Emerson on life and love."

Five minutes into reading the Emerson essay, the bell rang.

Day 2: Adding Aspirations and Money to the Mix

I asked students to read the passages they selected from "The Conduct of Life" that they thought best characterized Emerson's philosophy. Several students raised their hands and offered opinions. Among the phrases mentioned was one of my favorite Emerson quotes, "Beauty is the pilot of the young soul."

George raised his hand, "Every man is entitled to be valued by his best moment."

"You think that's what Emerson thinks about love and life?"

George smiled and said, "No, but that's a pretty cool quote."

"Yes, I like it too," I said. "How about this one: 'The secret of ugliness consists not in irregularity, but in being uninteresting.' What's Emerson mean by that?"

"You can be ugly, but still be interesting. Kind of like Drew Carey."

"He's cute."

"Right, a fat guy in big glasses is cute."

I said, "Perhaps he is interesting. How does Emerson's perspective compare with the views of Cohen, Shakespeare, and Young?"

"Emerson's more positive. He thinks we should all get along, that we are all connected."

"Fire is the most negative; Emerson and Shakespeare are the most positive. The guy who wrote about the rose is kind of in-between. The rose is beautiful, but it can still cut you up."

Carlyn said, "Emerson never really talks about love directly, but you get a feel for what he thinks about it, anyway."

I asked, "Where do you see that, Carlyn? Any particular line?"

Carlyn flipped through the handout, "At the beginning of the essay, he writes, 'The human heart concerns us more than the poring into microscopes, and is larger than can be measured by the pompous figures of an astronomer.' The human heart, love . . . it's the most important thing, not all these books and formulas."

"Great, Carlyn." I asked the class to get out a sheet of paper and to write down two things—a definition of love and an aspiration. I moved to the chalkboard and wrote the assignment. Carlyn rolled her eyes again.

a. Define love.
b. Describe at least one aspiration that you have for yourself for your lifetime (or at least over the course of the next two or three years).

I gave students several minutes to write out their definitions; then I asked for volunteers to read them out loud.

"Love is a tornado that rips across the insides of your heart, leaving either a path of destruction or a wake of flowers."

"Love is when your feelings are so strong, it hurts. When you would rather walk through hell than have that person be unhappy for any amount of time, that's love."

"Love is basically liking someone for a long period of time. I don't think that you can 'love' just one person. I believe love is something one chooses to do. Love is a choice."

"Love is like a black negligee. It starts out exciting and sexy, but over time becomes impractical and tacky."

"Love is a kind of friendship that makes you a better person."

Carlyn wrote, "Love is the unseen and unlooked for rock in the path that sends you flying off your bike."

The students' definitions were quite surprising—great fodder from which to work. I was setting them up for writing some poetry, though they didn't know it yet. Regarding their aspirations (part b of the assignment), the most popular response was money, "marry rich," though one student wanted to be an accountant and another wanted to be the world's first fat supermodel. Carlyn wrote, "My aspiration is to be fabulously wealthy and famous or at least really happy. Other than that, I haven't a clue."

Because of students' preoccupation with money, I handed out copies of "Nickel-and-Dimed," an article that I had clipped from a *Harper's Magazine* (Ehrenreich 1999). "Nickel-and-Dimed" is about a writer who moves to Key West to see if she can make ends meet via several minimum-wage jobs, such as housekeeper and waitress. The article was later expanded to a book (entitled *Nickel and Dimed*).

I said, "Many of you said that you wanted to marry rich. If that's really true, then aren't you giving a higher value to money than love?" I read the first page of "Nickel-and-Dimed" out loud, then the bell rang. "Finish this tonight and we'll talk about it tomorrow."

Day 3: Writing a Pantoum

From the discussion before the bell, I could tell that most students had actually read "Nickel-and-Dimed" (okay, except Jacob, who put his head on the desk and pretended to sleep). I could tell students had read it because they were talking about the life of a waitress and pointing out some curse words scattered throughout the essay.

I said, "Okay, so how does money affect the life of the author in 'Nickel-and-Dimed?'"

"She's pathetic. She's scrambling for whatever she can get."

"Doesn't she have to scramble so that she gets enough money to pay the bills?"

"Just get a better job."

The conversation was brisk and exciting, and I couldn't help but argue when I thought some students were becoming overly condescending and judgmental. Then I asked, "To what extent does the author of 'Nickel-and-Dimed' reject Emerson's notions of love, life, and happiness? To what extent does the author's viewpoint affirm Emerson's beliefs?" They had to think about this one, so I gave them a minute.

"You know, she kind of affirms Emerson in a way because she becomes friends with a lot of people and she's kind of happy doing her gross jobs. She is always tired and poor, but she has these friends who come through for her."

As the discussion intensified, I kept asking (in many different ways) about the role that money should play in life. I asked students to cite one or two of their favorite passages from the story (but they had to say "beep" whenever they came across a curse word). Then, we talked about their favorite characters—the cook, the manager, the friend, the dishwasher. I handed out two blank sheets of white paper to every student.

"Now I want you to draw something. You have two sheets in case you mess up on your first attempt. I want you to draw something that represents one of the following . . ." I turned to the chalkboard and wrote:

    a. Your personal perspective on love

    b. A personal philosophy of life

    c. The view toward love or the philosophy of life espoused by Emerson, Cohen, Shakespeare, Young, or any character from "Nickel-and-Dimed."

"We draw. That's it?" George asked. "I can draw anything I want?"

"Great. Drawing in English. Makes a lot of sense," Carlyn said.

"What are we supposed to draw?"

"Is this for a grade?"

I repeated the instructions louder, while pointing to the options on the board. "Remember your definition of love? You may want to draw something that represents that. Or you might be intrigued by Emerson's definition of love, or about the life philosophy of one of the characters in "Nickel-and-Dimed.""

Once students completed their drawings, I handed out a worksheet (Handout 6.2) that explained how to write a pantoum. "Now that you have a drawing, I want you to write a poem to accompany it." I went over the directions on the handout.

I like the pantoum because students usually are not familiar with it and the poem's structure allows much flexibility. In addition, the pantoum offers a format that students can readily understand and that requires them to think and write. For her drawing, Carlyn sketched a rose lying in an open hand. The rose had huge thorns on it and a bloody gash running through the area of the palm.

HANDOUT **6.2**

Writing a Pantoum

A pantoum is a form of poetry derived from fifteenth-century Malayan literature. Sometimes the poem rhymes, but rhyming lines are not required. The pattern of the poem is as follows:

    Line 1
    Line 2
    Line 3
    Line 4

    Line 5 (same as line 2)
    Line 6
    Line 7 (same as line 4)
    Line 8

    Line 9 (same as line 6)
    Line 10
    Line 11 (same as line 8)
    Line 12

Pantoum
by Carlyn Reichel

Beauty holds a hidden thorn,
For to tell a true war story
is to tell of love
in the dust of the floor.

To tell a true war story,
think only of man's heart
in the dust of the floor,
forget the corners no one sees.

Think only of man's heart
Bleeding life away for all the earth,
Don't forget the corners no one sees,
In hopes of velvet-petal comforts.

Bleeding life away for all the earth
'comes valiant in cities of reckless abandon,
But hopes of velvet-petal comforts
Fade into the pricks of wine-red roses.

Come valiant in cities of reckless abandon,
We await you there without fear;
Fade into the pricks of wine-red roses,
And those who cheer love will cheer for you:

Awaiting you there without fear
Is to tell of love,
And those who cheer love will cheer for you
But beauty holds a hidden thorn.

"Velvet-petal comforts." It was a helluva poem.

Day 4: Reading Life Philosophies of the Eminent

Each student recited their poem in class. While the individual student recited the poem, I carried around the accompanying drawing so that others could see the drawing as the poem was being read. We discussed each poem and I called attention to at least one powerfully written phrase in each student's poem. Several students read their poems more than once, sometimes at my request, sometimes at the request of a fellow student. As this was an oral, enabling exercise, I tried to point out only effective uses of language and turns of phrase. I wanted to build students up a bit before I challenged them with another assignment.

I divided students into groups of three or four. As students would be working in this group on a succession of assignments, I placed them in groups with great care. For this assignment, I asked groups to select a writer, speaker, and compiler. The compiler was responsible for finding evidence—at least two passages from the text. The compiler also made sure that nothing important got left out of the written summary or the oral presentation.

I handed out short chapters that explicated the personal philosophies of life of various individuals. I chose chapters by Jane Goodall, Albert Einstein, Jeanne Kirkpatrick, and Elie Wiesel from a book edited by Clifton Fadiman (*Living Philosophies*) as well as excerpts from Niccolo Machiavelli's *The Prince* and Marcus Aurelius' *Meditations*. I had copied chapters from a variety of writers—Aristotle, Plato, Martin Luther, Martin Luther King, Malcolm X, Susan B. Anthony, Booker T. Washington, Thomas Jefferson, and Carl Jung. I chose the individuals I did because I thought it possible that students knew few of them. I gave a complete set of handouts (six chapters) to every student, though their group had to read only one. I asked each group to announce when they had chosen the individual whose philosophy they wanted to read.

"Hey, is Goodall the monkey woman?"

I said, "Yes."

"We'll do her."

"Baines, who is this Marcus dude?"

I said, "Did you see the film *Gladiator*? Marcus was the smart, old, great emperor, played by Richard Harris."

"Okay, we'll do the *Gladiator* guy."

And so it went, until each group had selected an individual.

I said, "You are going to report to the class on the individual's philosophy of life, conception of love, and anything else that you think is interesting. And you need to cite at least one phrase in the selection to substantiate your contentions. Write everything out." I wrote on the board:

> Ascertain: (a) the individual's philosophy of life; (b) the individual's conception of love; (c) any other points of interest or unique insights.
> At least one phrase verbatim for a, one for b, and one for c.

The class began reading their selections. I said, "If you don't get through today, complete it tonight. I'll give you the first ten minutes of class tomorrow to compare notes before you have to present." The bell rang.

Day 5: Missed Opportunities—Jacob Checks Out

Groups presented their summaries of philosophies of life to the class. After each group presented, I asked several probing questions. I always asked for further evidence.

Although I don't do it often, I used the old "You might have to know this for a test" routine. "You may want to jot down these various philosophies in case you get asked about them on an exam sometime" (smile).

At the end of every student presentation, I tried to get the group to summarize briefly the writer's perspective without consulting any notes. Carlyn's group did Jeanne Kirkpatrick.

Carlyn's group (with Carrie and Lissette)

a. Life—Jeanne Kirkpatrick has changed from wanting to know answers to meeting her responsibilities and obligations. She much prefers fulfilling roles and expectations to being a seeker, someone constantly seeking to find the answers to the big questions. Evidence: "Commitments give meaning to life—commitments to family, country, friends, work, standards of civilized behavior, God—a meaningful life requires making and fulfilling commitments."

b. Love—begins and ends with the family and it endures forever. Real love must develop from good character. "Good character is a prerequisite to happiness. It entails empathy, courage, generosity, work, honesty, discipline, and balance." She thinks that a drug addict can't feel love because he is totally "self-centered and self-indulgent." According to Jeanne, a person has to have good character to know love.

c. Interesting—religion—She thinks that religion is what gives structure to life, though she doesn't seem too sold on some of the details of Christianity. I mean, I think her Christianity is pretty much up for grabs, though she goes to church and everything. It's like the religion itself isn't that important as much as it is that you follow some kind of moral guide. "No one, in my view, can entirely escape conditioning by his or her society." "Religions and their answers are also given in one's time and place. Christianity is the foundation of my civilization, and I am a Christian."

Because some of the chapters were quite difficult, I decided the class needed a little change of pace. So, I handed out a copy of Walt Whitman's poem "When I Heard the Learn'd Astronomer," a poem that makes a case for enjoying the beauty of nature without overanalyzing it.

Instead of overanalyzing "Astronomer," I asked students what phrases in the poem they found particularly effective.

"He uses tired and sick rather than sick and tired."

"Perfect silence."

"Mystical moist night-air."

I asked, "What if someone offered you a million bucks after you graduated from high school. What would you do?"

"Take it."

"Depends on what they wanted me to do."

"For a million bucks, I'd do just about anything. You do it, then it's over. You still got the million."

I handed out "Shooting Star," a nonfiction article from *The New Republic* (Grann 2000), and said, "'Shooting Star' is about a high school student named Leon Smith who was drafted to play professional basketball." As if on cue, there was a knock on the door. I went to the door and found Jacob there, smiling.

"I'm checking out, sir," he said.

"You're kidding, aren't you, Jacob?"

"I ain't no schoolboy."

When I Heard the Learn'd Astronomer
by Walt Whitman

When I heard the learn'd astronomer
When the proofs, the figures, were ranged in columns before me,
When I was shown the charts, the diagrams, to add, divide, and measure them,
When I sitting heard the astronomer where he lectured with much applause
*   in the lecture-room,*
How soon unaccountable I became tired and sick,
Till rising and gliding out I wander'd off by myself,
In the mystical moist night-air, and from time to time,
Look'd up in perfect silence at the stars.

"If you don't graduate from high school, it's going to be really hard for you to get into college."

"I ain't going to college. Can't afford it."

Jacob fished in his pants pocket and pulled out a crumpled withdrawal slip. I opened the door and walked over to my desk. A few class members called out to him. George said, "What you doing, fool?" Jacob smiled and fidgeted.

I looked over my gradebook. Jacob had failed every grading period except the first, when he had to stay eligible for football. This term, he had been absent nine days already, though the five grades I had for him came to a 72. He had failed for the year, anyway, so I thought, "What the heck, let's leave a good taste in his mouth," decided not to average in the zeros, and scribbled out "72" for the term.

"You sure you want to leave now? Hey, we're just starting to read about Leon Smith, this guy who was drafted for the NBA when he was still in high school." I handed Jacob a copy of the article.

"That's okay. Never give up, huh Baines?" Jacob smiled, picked up his signed withdrawal form, and crammed it back into his pants pocket. He put the article back on my desk, looked at George, nodded, and said, "Later."

I was depressed, so stood at my desk for a moment and stared at the wall. I looked up at the clock and noticed that there were only five minutes left in class. While the class whispered about Jacob's departure, I wrote on the board:

a. What is Leon's philosophy of life?

b. What is Leon's conception of love?

c. What are some other unique attributes with regard to Leon Smith's life?

"Read this tonight. You can meet with your groups to discuss the answers to the questions in the first ten minutes of tomorrow. As you read, try to find evidence, evidence, evidence." The bell rang and I thought about Jacob, a lazy eighteen-year-old kid who read about as well as most fourth graders, who loathed writing, and who would have to face the world without a high school diploma. Not the end of the world, but not very auspicious either.

I had devoted much time to working with Jacob on his reading and writing, but often he simply refused to pick up the pencil or come to class. I sincerely believe that if I had had enough time and had punched the correct buttons, I could have reached Jacob. But, I likely would not have had enough left over to teach anyone else or to have a life of my own. At least, that's what I told myself.

Day 6: Money and Morality

As promised, I gave students ten minutes at the beginning of class to discuss their answers and write down responses. The subject of "Shooting Star" was Leon Smith, a teenager from a poor Chicago slum who played in the city leagues and for a private Catholic high school, and who went to a summer basketball camp in New Jersey. Voted MVP of the camp, the eighteen-year-old Smith was signed in the first round by the Dallas Mavericks of the NBA for a million and a half dollars. Before he played his first game, Leon fought with the coach and his teammates, was twice arrested by the police, and was abandoned by his girlfriend. By the end of the article, Smith has been put on waivers and is living in a cheap apartment in Houston, Texas, hoping for another chance.

During the class discussion, students focused on Smith's volatile temper. When his girlfriend dumped him, he tried to give her $30,000. When she still wouldn't take him back, he busted out the windows on her mother's car with his bare hands.

"You can't really compare Smith to any of the philosophers. He just kind of lived moment to moment. Didn't really think. Just reacted."

"A guy gets his hands on a million and blows it."

"Give me a million, dude, and I'll run laps. Man, I'd even clean my room."

During the discussion, I tried to point out the advantages of having a philosophy of life that helped you get through those tough moments in life when it feels like you are all alone in the world. In the story, Leon seemed to have lost control of his life when he fell into money. Again, I raised the possibility that money might not necessarily bring happiness, but many students would have none of it.

"You depressed and have nothing to do, you'd still rather sit in a nice, leather chair than on some stinky cardboard box."

"Better to be heartbroken and rich than heartbroken and poor."

"You drive around in a nasty old car, ain't nobody going out with you, anyway."

I said, "Okay, okay. I know you think money is important. But some things money just can't buy—integrity, for example."

George said, "You pay me. I'll do it."

I said, "Let's step back for a minute, okay? Let's take an inventory of the work you have done thus far. Bring all your papers and all the handouts to class with you tomorrow. You will need them all for a forthcoming assignment that has to do with producing a video. By the way, how many of you can get access to a camcorder for a class assignment?"

I was lucky enough to have five students who said that they could bring in camcorders. With my own old camcorder for a backup, we were in business. I didn't even need to borrow any from the librarian or head coach. "Please ask your parent or guardian if you can bring them to school. Then try to bring them in tomorrow, okay?"

The effect of money on student morality had me a bit worried. So, I looked among my handouts for something that might bring the dilemma into focus. I found a contemporary short story called "Three Thousand Dollars" (Lipsky 1992) about a young man who lies to both his mother and father so that he may have a more "hassle-free" life. I grabbed copies of "Three Thousand Dollars," handed them out, and said, "Okay, here's a story about Richard, a kid in college whose parents are divorced. He plays his dad against his mom for money. Read it by the beginning of next class. As you read the story, think about the trade-off that Richard makes—money for ethics. Locate and write down the one sentence that best reflects Richard's view on life."

On the board, I wrote, "Read 'Three Thousand Dollars.' Find the sentence that best reflects Richard's (main character's) view on life."

Day 7: Sell Out

Before class began, I stood at the door and reminded students as they walked in, "You're going to need all your handouts and assignments today." Most students remembered them, though George said that he had to go back to his locker and get a few things. "Okay," I said. "Just hurry up."

When George returned, I asked students several questions about "Three Thousand Dollars." I said, "So, what's the most important sentence?"

"'I'm your mother, and you're supposed to be my burden.'"

"What would upset mom now is not only the money—although the money would be a big part of it—but also that I tried to put something over on her."

I tried to tie up the discussion, but it was messy. Most students acknowledged that, like Richard, they had lied to get a little spare change and would not hesitate to do it again if the situation presented itself. Depressing.

I asked students to get out their notebooks. I recapped what students had done thus far. They had read the life philosophies of Emerson, Machiavelli, Kirkpatrick, Aurelius, Goodall, and Wiesel. They had written a poem reflective of their (or a character's or writer's) philosophy of life and had read and analyzed two works of nonfiction ("Nickel-and-Dimed" and "Shooting Star") in relation to how a person's culture, family, and social class influence life and love. They had read the poetry of Shakespeare, Whitman, Young, and Cohen and read a short story involving ethics, choices, and decisions.

I said, "Now you are going to write (a) a personal philosophy of life, perception of love or thoughts on beauty or (b) a short story that illustrates your personal philosophy of life. Use the material in your notebook for inspiration. Cite passages from any of the articles, stories, or poems we've covered. You may eventually adapt your essay or story for film. Thus, make your essays or stories at least two pages, but less than twenty." On the board, I wrote, "Write an essay or short story describing your philosophy of life or love. 2–20 pages." Then I handed out the grading scale (Handout 6.4).

I said, "Any questions?"

George asked, "How long does it have to be?"

I pointed to the board and said, "Make it great, something that really expresses what you feel and think about life. It can be a story, like 'Three Thousand Dollars,' or it can be an essay like those chapters we read last week by Kirkpatrick, Wiesel, and those folks."

Carlyn said, "Like this grading scale really helps. What, you count off 50 points if you don't think my language is 'vibrant'?"

I said, "No, Carlyn. For you, nonvibrant language would mean minus 60." That got her eyes really moving. I'm not sure, but I thought I saw a little grin appear at the corner of her mouth. Touché.

Day 8: Students Write Their Philosophies of Life (or Love)

I opened class with a quote from the Buddha:

> Come, people, do not base your life on what others tell you, nor upon tradition, nor upon rumor, nor upon scripture, nor upon surmise, nor upon axioms, nor upon specious reasoning, nor upon some bias, nor upon someone's apparent talents, nor upon the authority of a teacher. Instead, when you yourselves know 'These things are good, these things are worthy, these things are wise, these things lead to happiness and well-being,' then you should go ahead and live life accordingly. (From the Sutra of the Kalamas, AN III.65, interpreted)

Then, I said, "I want you to work all day today on writing your philosophies of life or love. Tomorrow, they are due at the beginning of class. If you need some help, just raise your hand and I'll come over. Otherwise, I'll not disturb you."

HANDOUT **6.4**

Evaluation for Short Story or Essay Describing Your Philosophy of Life

A = higher order thinking, artistically rendered, compellingly argued, vibrant use of language

C = adequate thought, addresses components, average arguments, evident writing skills

Papers whose quality places them between the descriptions of A and C will receive a B. Papers that fall below expectations for a C will receive D or F.

Students groaned, but most seemed to jump into the assignment. I only had to walk by George's desk six or seven times to keep him on task. Carlyn had moved to a corner of the room and was in a writing fury. I answered a few questions, but most of the time, the only sound you could hear was pen scrawling on paper.

Day 9: CIS Editing; Jumpstarting the Video

I asked students to read their essays aloud within their groups. Following is Carlyn's initial paper.

Moon Faces
by Carlyn Reichel

For sixteen years, I have looked at the moon and never seen the man residing there. I've heard he has a pet rabbit, but I've never found that either. I had never counted myself inferior to the average four year old until last night. I woke up around 4 a.m. and found I could not get back to sleep, something that has never happened before. I laid in bed and looked out into the night, hoping the crickets would lull me back to dreams, and again examined the familiar surface of the lucent moon in a twinkling sky.

My room has a wall of windows, open to the sky, perfect for such late night investigations. The reflected light of night washes over my bed to the recesses of my room. In this way, I noticed the delicate beauty ordinary objects take on in soft moon glow, the mystery this hides in the faintest shadow, the quality that makes children fear closet monsters, enchants artists and inspires lovers. I laid awake, listening for some sign of dawn when I would inevitably fall back asleep. Searching for some sign of life in the deep ridges and valleys of Phoebe's countenance, I came to the horrible realization that it was not alive. In spite of all the beauty and marvel of the ages encompassed by its sphere, the man did not possess life, at least not in the way I do (if life can truly be possessed.) The cold rationality of this thought saddened me, and alone with the moon and my thoughts, I tried to think of what life means to me.

One thing is clear to me above all else, life is purposeful. If my life and everyone else's was just random, chaotic patterns of happenstance, the futility of it would overcome everyone. Instead, we are born with an ingrained drive to achieve some intangible goal that will fill our lives with meaning, order, and hope. This is our passion, our mission, and our purpose in life. In order to be a contributing member of society, we must therefore find and follow our passion in life. Like the honeybee that fulfills its purpose unwittingly by doing what it is driven to do, gather pollen for honey, we must strive to be not only "on purpose" conventional standards, but "on passion" according to our own, and the rest will follow. In fulfilling ourselves, we help fulfill the world as a whole.

Because of this, everyone is different and uniquely gifted; the key comes in finding a unity through diversity in which everyone is willing to step into their custom designed roles for the good of everyone else. As is inscribed above the Temple of

Apollo at Delphi, the most basic philosophy for my life is "Know Thyself." If we know strengths, weaknesses, abilities, loves, hates, etc., then we are comfortable to take the risks of life, with certainty of good times ahead, and joining the interwoven web connecting each man to his brother and sister by the human condition.

And if one major passion is fulfilled, do not all others fall in line as well? No. The intricacies of life are still a tossup most times; it keeps us original. Certainly new opportunities and aspirations follow in the wake of "the big one," but these are mostly just the rotted out planks of civilization trying to keep us civilized in a changing world. The only constant we have is our overall goal, our purpose, which forms the floor we stand on; it is our one support, and all others are merely superfluous ornamentations that may improve the surroundings, but add nothing.

The most ridiculous frill we cling to is love, the roof and some say pinnacle of our creation. However, love in and of itself is mostly useless, made special only when shared. One can get along fine without love. Machiavelli even said "it is safer to be feared than loved," so why waste the time? The truth of the matter is that while fear might be "safer" than love, it is definitely not better. Pure love, true love, is the one flawless creation of mankind; it's what separates us from the animals in many respects. The kind of love we desire though is Hollywood love, created by the media and mass distributed with the help of Nike and Gatorade. Fake, and therefore useless.

If life is a house, with walls of civilized expectations and dreams, a ceiling of love, and a floor of passion, then religion is the nails that hold it all together. To be accepting of something larger than oneself is key not only in mental stability, but also in overall contentment. Life is too much for one person to hold together without help, but to make that statement of faith is to acknowledge we need not struggle alone. As Martin Luther asserted nearly 500 years ago, it is by grace alone, faith alone, and scripture alone that we are saved.

So, one late night, I laid awake in my bed and thought about life as I waited to hear the crack of dawn. One of my most final conclusions was that I can't answer the biggest questions in life, and truthfully, I don't think I would want to. Something mysterious should always be left just far enough out of the moonlight to scare and excite us.

I looked again and over the moon to see the truth hidden there that night, and finally realized that while the moon may not be alive, it is certainly following its passion and staying on purpose. Nightly it rains deepened sunlight on the deprived earth, nightly it inspires poets and dreamers, nightly it watches over the romantics with its gentle nurturing and even unseen it wields great force over the tides. If this is true, then the moon possesses far more life than many aimless humans do. When I eventually drifted off into sleep again that night, I was smiling because after sixteen years, I realized I had finally seen the man in the moon.

I asked each student in the group to offer constructive comments. Then, I asked each student to choose a partner. The partner was to read the paper and fill out the peer editing worksheet (Handout 6.5).

Students read each others' papers and critiqued them using steps a–f. Following is Carrie's response to Carlyn's paper.

HANDOUT **6.5**

CIS (Colors, Images, Sounds)
Peer Editing Worksheet

   a. What are the dominant colors (might be implicit)?

   b. Write at least two memorable images.

   c. What music (a specific song, such as "God Bless America," or a kind of music—traditional, country and western, rock, classical) does the paper bring to mind?

   d. Point out at least one area that needs improvement (perhaps some vague or contradictory wording, egregious errors of syntax or semantics, or other problem). Suggest how to make the area that needs improvement stronger.

   e. Denote at least one area that is particularly effective.

   f. Make suggestions relative to turning the essay or story into a film.

CIS (Colors, Images, and Sounds) Peer Editing Worksheet
Carrie's Response to Carlyn's Paper

a. silver   grey
    red   black
    blue
    white

b. the moon from behind an open window
    a busy street with people in business suits walking to work
    a house of wood—single board with a nail in it
    the Hollywood sign
    honeybee going from one flower to another

c. sound of crickets
    melody of a lullaby

d. The moon is following his passion and staying on purpose? I'm not sure what you mean. The moon follows his (or is it a her?) orbit as the laws of nature say he must?

e. I like this line—The most ridiculous frill we cling to is love, the roof and some say pinnacle of our creation.

f. Need cool pictures of the moon and pictures at night for a film.

    I like CIS peer editing because it gets students out of the habit of writing, "Best paper I've ever read. A+" on every paper they read. Instead, the CIS gets students out of their knee-jerk evaluative responses and asks them to cite specific parts of a paper, including aspects that may not have occurred to the author. After students listened to each others' writing and peer edited with a partner, the group voted on which essay or story they wanted to film. They could base the video on one essay/story or combine papers from two or more students into one production. I said, "By the beginning of class tomorrow, I want you to announce which paper(s) your group is going to use as the basis for the video." The negotiation among groups was highly interactive and animated. Students read and reread papers with the seriousness of an editor pondering next month's issue.

Life was good.

Day 10: Writing the Screenplay and Developing a Shooting Schedule

The first item of business was counting up the number of camcorders students brought in. When I asked students if they remembered to bring them, I heard two or three comments along the lines of "Oh yeah," and "Man, I knew there was something. . . ." It turned out that three students had remembered to bring their camcorders. Not bad. I asked the two students who forgot to please remember to bring their camcorders tomorrow.

The chapter on screenwriting (Chapter 4) contains many pointers for shooting with cheap camcorders on a budget of zero, so I won't belabor those points again here. Suffice it to say that I advocate students rely heavily on "head shots" (shots in which the individual's head almost fills the frame), and I emphasize that the sound should be comprehensible. Students must turn in a working screenplay with their videos. Today in class, I asked students to discuss how and where they will shoot the video, who will star in the video, and other details. As in the screenwriting experience, I recommend giving students in each group a role—director/editor, lead actor, writer, and cameraperson/sound engineer.

I showed students how to make titles without fancy equipment. I asked George to write a short phrase from one of his articles on a sheet of paper. "But write big so that it fills up the page, okay?"

George looked through his notes, then painstakingly wrote, "Every man is entitled to be valued by his best moment." I taped George's piece of notebook paper against the wall, got out my Sony camcorder, and zoomed in on it. Then, I plugged the camcorder into the television and showed the class. "See how easy it is to make titles. Use your imagination. You don't need any fancy special effects. Homemade titles are the best."

Because the groups were abuzz with discussions on what and how to film, I waited until the last fifteen minutes of class for their commitments. I went around and asked every group to explain their idea for a video. Three groups decided to adapt a single paper, but the other two groups decided to combine aspects from the papers of all group members.

I said, "You should begin planning where and when you will shoot the video. Your grade will be based upon the quality of the film as an independent project, without regard to the degree of its adherence to the original paper (or other criteria). But, for now, I want you to turn in your papers to me, so that I can write comments on them before you start filming. After I turn them back to you on Monday, you can begin writing the screenplay. Everyone must turn in a working screenplay with the video."

Day 11: Bolstering the Image

I spent most of the weekend reading papers, but it was worth it. The papers represented solid efforts from most students. Even George turned in something. More good news: The two students with the camcorders had remembered to bring them. So, every group had access to a camcorder.

I handed back the essays at the beginning of class. I had written extensive comments with regard to:

a. Content ("Your insight that night both frightens and liberates you is a compelling thought. I still prefer a nightlight even at my age . . .")
b. Grammar, spelling, language, and syntax ("You use the word *it* twelve times in two paragraphs. Rather than overusing *it*, perhaps you could write out the word to which *it* refers.")
c. Style ("You write 'he is not alive,' which is not as powerful as other possibilities—'the moon is a gray, frozen rock,' for example").

George was in a group that included a very smart, musically talented, artistic student named Brady. Brady had written an avante-garde short story about a painter who painted landscapes and objects that would come to life. Over time, the main character begins to inhabit the landscapes and then the landscapes start taking over the real world. It was a disturbing, but creative, effort. On my comments to Brady, I praised his vision and asked him several questions concerning how his group planned to film it. I wrote, "You'll have to think of a way to get the drawings to come to life. Your special-effects budget is somewhat limited." Brady suggested to the group that they abandon his idea, but the group argued for it. The group wound up staying with the idea, though they acknowledged that they would have to do some rewriting.

I handed out the evaluation sheet for the film (Handout 6.6).

I said, "For the still shots of the group, I'm going to bring my Polaroid camera tomorrow and take your photo. So, you can put that somewhere in your video. If you wind up taking a group's photo, get a close-up. I only want to see faces in the photograph."

Then, I brought thirty or so large coffee-table books on art and photography, including *The Meaning of Life* and *More Reflections on the Meaning of Life* (Friend 1991, 1992), which contain a wide array of quotations and stunning photographs. I showed the students some of my favorite photographs and read them some quotations from *The Meaning of Life*. Students rummaged through the books for the remainder of the period, often pausing to write down quotations or to note the page number of a particularly interesting image.

HANDOUT **6.6**

Film Evaluation

Films must contain the following elements:

a. Opening credits.
b. Shot of a photograph of the individuals in the group.
c. At least one other still shot.
d. Artsy, creative visuals.
e. Audible voice and sound.
f. Good framing (you are close enough to the subject to see what is going on).
g. Quality of story or essay.
h. Must contain at least two quotations from writers, philosophers, or poets (may be done as part of the dialogue or soundtrack or you may shoot a still of the quotation written out).
i. Must contain at least one piece of music (you may separately record an audio-cassette to play simultaneously with the video). Original compositions and sound effects are encouraged.
j. Closing credits.
k. Extra credit for anyone who turns their film into a musical or opera.

Days 12 to 19 (add up to two days if necessary): Polaroids

When the bell rang, most students were already deeply involved in discussing their videos. I brought out my Polaroid and showed students how to take a photo with it. I said, "Get real close and press the big, red button. Someone other than a group member has to take your photo because you have to all be in it. Remember, somehow you have to fit in a photo of all group members in your video."

Students spent the remainder of the class periods shooting video and mapping out their ideas. I put together three crude editing suites (two VCRs and a monitor) and told students that I would be happy to check out a VCR if they needed to edit at home. Most groups planned to get together over the weekend to edit and didn't use the editing suites.

Because I wanted to give students plenty of time to shoot and edit, I made the due date for the video more than a week away. During the next week, the class worked on other assignments, though if students finished their work early, I allowed them to work on their videos.

Day 20 (add a day if necessary): Presentations

On the day of the presentations, I made a few guidelines.

I said, "Just show us the video without any prefacing. Save your stories and bloopers for after all the presentations. Then, we'll have an open discussion where you can share your trials, victories, and bloopers with each other. Take your time getting set up. Of course, after you have seen all the presentations, I want you to rate them, from best to worst. I don't want you to rate them based upon friends you might have in the class, but on who you think has made the most compelling film. You cannot rate your own."

Students showed their videos. To make the student presentations as theater-like as possible, I borrowed an LCD projector. I plugged the VCR into the LCD and cast the video against one of the white walls in the classroom, producing a huge image. I had a CD/cassette player ready to go for those who needed one.

I handed out the video evaluation sheets. "This is what you should use to rate the videos. Based upon these criteria, what group produced the best video?"

The group who combined parts of every member's essay into a single screenplay went first. Theirs was a delightful film that expressed each of their philosophies of love. They included interviews with parents, photos of their boyfriends over the years, several outstanding quotations from Emerson, Shakespeare, and Wiesel, and footage of each of them espousing excerpts from their original essays on the nature of love.

From what I could tell, George did most of the camerawork in his group and helped with editing. Instead of having drawings come to life, his group took drawings and flowers and other objects and set them on fire. These images were interspersed with heavily philosophic quotes from Nietzsche, Freud, Machiavelli, and Kurt Cobain (deceased vocalist of the rock band Nirvana). During the post-film discussion, Brady said, "The premise is the same for the film as for the artist whose drawings come to life. The only difference is that instead of reality being taken over by imaginary drawings, reality goes up in flames."

Carlyn's group created a very interesting video, replete with clips from the commercial films *Mulan, Steel Magnolias, Braveheart, The Muppet Movie,* and *Angel*; quotations from Thoreau, Confucius, and Emerson; and artwork by Rodin, Picasso, Matisse, and Munch.

Day 21: From Image to Word

Before class, George said, "Hey, I saw Jacob the other day."

I asked, "Really? What's he doing?"

"Saw him at the gas station filling up his dad's car. He said that he's just sitting around the house taking it easy, mostly. His dad is trying to get him to try for a job at the body shop where he works."

"Jacob going to do that?"

"Probably. He doesn't have anything else going on."

"He doing okay?"

"Yeah, he's fine. Same old good-for-nothing Jacob."

I asked students to reacquaint themselves with previous assignments—the definition of love, the pantoum, and the initial essay or story—in light of their video.

I said, "I want you to rewrite your initial essay or story, considering my editorial comments and those of your group done before the shooting of the video. I want you to imbue your paper with a sense of the content and style of the film. This sheet of paper explicates exactly what I want you to do." I gave them Handout 6.7.

For his revision, George translated his original story into a screenplay. I tried not to make a big deal out of George going beyond the contours of the assignment, but I felt like pumping my fist in the air and yelling, "All right!" George's revision was bleak and pessimistic and riddled with errors, spelling mostly. Basically, the plot revolves around a guy who walks around a town smoking a cigarette. He meets a bunch of people—a lying minister, a harsh teacher, and a bullying policeman. They have short conversations with him, say a few despicable things, then end by saying, "Have a nice day." The main character frowns and says, "Ain't nothing nice about it."

Even if it wasn't the greatest screenplay ever written, George had written eleven pages, a world record for him. Of course, his favorite quote, "Every man is entitled to be valued by his best moment," made it into his story as well. They are the words uttered by the main character just before he gets run over (fatally) by a car in the final scene.

HANDOUT **6.7**

From Sensory Input Back to Words

Revise your original paper. If you shot a screenplay from your script, your assignment is straightforward. You try to integrate aspects of the video into your original paper. This should include at a minimum the following components:

a. At least two images from the film.
b. A sense of the music and soundtrack.
c. Any ideas that have been lurking in your head that you found difficult to film or that have become manifest since you finished the original draft.

If your essay or story was *not* filmed, you have a little more leverage. You should include at a minimum:

a. At least two images from art books or books of photography that are compatible with your paper. Make copies of the images and include them with your paper.
b. Communicate some sense of music. There are infinite ways of doing this. You might describe how a piece of music fits with your philosophy of life or love, add a musical lilt to your writing (you may want to use an epic poem such as "Rime of the Ancient Mariner" for a model), or have a character sing or speak lyrics from a song.
c. If an idea has come to you in the process of filming the video, or if aspects of your philosophy of life/love have changed, you may want to explore the idea in this paper.

For her revision, Carlyn significantly revised her original philosophy of life paper, incorporating several images, songs, and quotations from her group's video. Her final paper follows.

Night Watches
by Carlyn Reichel

By the light of garish day, our lives are ordered. With meteoric rising and falling of the sun, so also go the fevered ambitions, the torrid loves, the infectious beauties of most standardized existences, and after dark these wretched souls lose themselves in the empty morass that consumes the inner crevices of their most true selves. Without one blinding star to lead them, they are dull to the twinkling multitude that emerge to dance only after Apollo has reined in his chariot for the day. They fear the night and its hosts of heaven, for it is in the darkness that our truest selves are revealed. Without the light to shield our eyes, we cannot hide from our most innate nature. There is no mask on the prayers we utter to our secret gods in the night, no curtain to draw before our most cutthroat desires, no prop of civilization left to keep us in line when the wolves that roam our souls howl with their brothers after business hours. This thought terrifies, maddens, conquers the shining citizen of the day who comes to fear his own shadow.

The most free souls revel in the night, for with the darkness comes the unknown, the mysterious, and therefore, the exciting. In the night, true discoveries of the most important kind can be made, discoveries in oneself. Obstacles, character, goals are all transformed to genuine proportions during the nocturnal hours, brought down from the daunting exaggerations of the day to scaleable height. However, this perspective is missed by those who would strike fires in the darkness as temporary markers, reminders of their predetermined course, but reminders that cast misrepresentative shadows and obscure the truth. They cannot see because the light has blinded them; they are immune to the indefinite shades that lie between the deepest blue and the starkest black.

The night is my element. I have always found it easier to stay awake into the small hours of the morning than to awaken with the morning star. I am comfortable there. As a child, shaded by the earth, I would converse with the stars until I could not listen to them any more. Although I knew them all by name, well my names at least (Winken, Blinken, Nod, and Fred), my love affair was with the moon. The moon and I, we had great times together, marvelous adventures, and not a care in the world until He inevitably fell, or more accurately, was pushed out of the sky. Even when I only slept the long hours away, the moon kept steady in His silent watch. For years I attended the moon, examining each ridge and valley that creased His face with the tender attention of a best friend, but pragmatism always kept my foot far enough away from the brink to allow me to pull back at any time. Its simple manifestation was that I could not see the man in the moon. The cold, calculating reason of the light prevented me from ever getting beyond the basic realities: the moon is not alive, He is stone and dust, frozen, barren, unresponsive. Night after night I looked for a face for my friend, but He continued to hide it from me in a cloud of rationality. I would lie awake, listening for and dreading the earsplitting crack of dawn, desperately searching for an eye, a mouth, some sign of life from the deep ridges and valleys I had memorized, anything. It was not there.

It began to seem like one big lie to me. Instead of revealing the truth perhaps darkness had continually hidden it from me. How could ordinary objects take on such a delicate beauty in soft moon glow without a life to originate it? What power could conceal mystery in the faintest shadow, inspire children to fear closet monsters, enchant artists, and enkindle lovers without heartbeat? As each question remained unanswered night after night, I lost hope, and, with great sadness, I bade Winken, Blinken, Nod, Fred, and the rest farewell and retreated to the light. At least the daylight brought answers, even if they were hollow and plain.

Now I am sixteen, and I have not been back yet. I cringe to be alone in the darkness without a torch to guide me on my way, and I chase the sun from first light to fading sunset. I have never told anyone about my inability to see the face proffered at my window each night, most nights now I'm too tired to even look anymore, but a part of me still counts myself inferior to the average four year old who can easily distinguish not only the man in the moon, but his pet rabbit as well.

But now I am also beginning to wonder if life is really as simple as the question of a heartbeat or a soul, if there is truly anybody out there. Certainly there are plenty of soulless people who are very much alive, and there are many soulful inanimates that lack the pleasantries of a pulse. Perhaps there should be a better qualifying factor determined. In all my teenage wisdom, one thing is clear to me above all else: life is purposeful. If life was just random, chaotic patterns of chance and luck, futility would overcome the will to exist. Instead, we are each born with an ingrained drive to achieve some intangible goal that will fill our lives with meaning, order, and hope. This is the passion, mission, and purpose of life. In order to be a contributing, soulful, alive member to society, I believe we must find and follow our passion in life. To create meaning for our life, we must not only be "on purpose" by conventional standards, but "on passion" in accordance with our own. The rest will follow.

In fulfilling ourselves, we are filling our place in the plan and fulfilling an obligation to the world. Because of this, everyone is different and uniquely gifted. Our goal should then be to step up and implement these gifts to find a unity of mankind through all diversity. However, we cannot expect to satisfy our roles in the world without an intimate knowledge of ourselves, otherwise we are just shadows playing at life. Mere shades of what our potential allows. If we know our strengths, weaknesses, loves, hates, then we are confident enough to brave the risks of life, with the certainty of good times ahead, and join the interwoven web connecting each man to his brother and sister of human condition.

If we are fortunate enough to discover our passion and become living members of the body human, all other wants and needs may not necessarily be immediately satisfied. The intricacies of life are still a tossup most times, subject to change at any moment and constantly affected by those around us; it keeps us original. Certainly new aspirations and opportunities follow in the wake of "the big one," but these are mostly just the rotted out planks of civilization trying to keep us civilized in a changed world by constantly reminding us that others are watching and judging. The only constant we have is our overall goal, our purpose, which forms the very floor we stand on. It is our one support, and all others are merely superfluous ornamentations that may briefly improve the surroundings, but add nothing.

The most ridiculous frill we cling to is love, the roof and some say pinnacle of our creation. However, love in and of itself is mostly useless as it is only made special when shared. One can get along fine without love, and Machiavelli even claimed "it is safer to be feared than loved." This is unbearably true as love can only lead to pain when it must inevitably end, but while it is far safer to harbor fear than love, it is by no means better. Pure love, true love, is the one flawless gift and creation of mankind; it is what separates us from the animals in many respects. The kind of love we desire though is adulterated with lust, jealousy, and control. It is Hollywood love, manufactured between strangers by illusions and directors, and mass distributed with the help of Nike and Gatorade. In a word, fake, and therefore useless.

In the structure of life, religion is the nails that holds everything together in place and allows us to function smoothly. Having an acceptance of something larger than oneself is key not only to mental stability, but also to overall contentment. Life is too much for one person, but to make a statement of faith is to acknowledge that we need not struggle alone. As Martin Luther asserted nearly 500 years ago, it is by grace alone, by faith alone, and by scripture alone that we are saved.

In writing down my beliefs, I think it is safe to say that I can not answer the biggest questions in life, and I do not think that I would want to. Some things mysterious should always be left just far enough out of the moonlight to scare and excite us.

As I look again at the countenance of the still-friendly moon, I think I have finally realized that there may be more truth behind the story of the man than I ever could accept as a child. He may not be alive, He may be an inanimate orb or cold indifference circling the planet, but He certainly is following His passion and staying on purpose. Nightly, He rains deepened sunlight on a cowering earth, nightly he inspires poets and dreamers, nightly He watches over the romantics with His gentle nurturing; the moon possesses more life than do the many aimless humans who cower in the glaring light and refuse to know themselves. I do not need to find a face in the shadows to assure me there is a man in the moon, I have always known in the dark. Perhaps as I teeter on the verge of adulthood, it is time for me to become better acquainted with myself, determine my passion, and step up to fulfill my place in the world. Perhaps it is again time for me to converse with Winken and Blinken. Perhaps it is time for me to turn off the glow of my computer screen, snuff out the halogen lamp, and step back into the darkness with open arms. Sweet Dreams.

Rather than simply go through the motions, Carlyn gave the revision of her paper her genuine best effort. She went beyond her usual perfunctory performance and put her heart and soul into expressing what she believed. It seems to me a teacher can ask for no more and that we settle too often for far less.

REFERENCES

General

Boeree, G. (2002). "Buddha." From *How to Get a Life,* Baines, L. and McBrayer, D. eds., book in preparation.
Emerson, R. (2000). *The Essential Writings of Ralph Waldo Emerson.* New York: Modern Library.

Books

Aurelius, M. (2000). *Meditations.* New York: Penguin.

    A deep, searching book elucidating aspects of the Stoic philosophy, but with an uncommonly insightful global perspective that values nature, humanism, and nobility of purpose.

Emerson, R. (1957). "The Conduct of Life." In P. Miller, ed. *The American Transcendentalists.* Garden City, New York: Doubleday: 171–186.

    In this essay, Emerson opens with a poem about a man who finds himself "happier to die for Beauty, than live for bread" (p. 172), then gradually explains his organic, tolerant, spiritual philosophy of life. Nuggets of wisdom abound in these few pages—"the secret of ugliness consists not in irregularity, but in being uninteresting" (p. 183); "Beauty without grace is the hook without the bait" (p. 182); " 'Tis curious that we only believe as deep as we live" (p. 173).

Fadiman, C., ed. (1990). *Living Philosophies.* New York: Doubleday.

    The following chapters from Fadiman's collection were used as handouts for "Conduct of Life," and the annotations are taken from students' papers.

    Albert Einstein, "From Living Philosophies," 3–6.

        Einstein advises that we shouldn't ponder life, just live it. Along the way, we should seek goodness, beauty, and truth. He feels that, in his lifetime, he stole most of what he knew and did from others who lived before him. According to Einstein, ultimate beauty is shrouded in mystery.

    Jane Goodall, "Respect for Life," 81–88.

        Goodall confesses that she didn't believe in God until her husband died. After that event, she believed that a spirit continues to live after death, so she acquired a belief in fate and believes that spirit or God is also evident in the lives of animals. Goodall thinks that the worst way to go through life is trying to be cool. A person should be fearless in expressing himself/herself to effect change and keep a reverence for all living things.

    Jeanne Kirkpatrick, "Making Sense," 152–160.

        Jeanne Kirkpatrick has changed from wanting to know answers to meeting her responsibilities and obligations. Love begins and ends with the family and it endures forever. She much prefers fulfilling roles and expectations to being a seeker, someone constantly seeking to find the answers to the big questions. She thinks that religion is what gives structure to life, though she doesn't seem too sold on some of the details of Christianity. I mean, I think her Christianity is pretty much up for grabs, though she goes to church and everything. It's like the religion itself isn't that important as much as it is that you follow some kind of moral guide.

    Elie Wiesel, "From One Generation to Another," 182–186.

        Wiesel's philosophy of life developed from his experiences with the Holocaust. He seems obsessed over why he remained alive while all his friends perished. Wiesel believes that a person shouldn't allow history or memory to impede his/her goals or enjoyment of life.

Friend, D., ed. (1991). *The Meaning of Life.* Boston: Little, Brown.

    A book containing compelling photographs and quotations from noted and obscure thinkers and writers.

———. (1992). *More Reflections on the Meaning of Life.* Boston: Little, Brown

    The sequel to the preceding book, containing compelling photographs and quotations from both noted and obscure thinkers and writers. Every bit as good as the first volume.

Machiavelli, N. (1998). *The Prince.* London: Oxford University Press.

    Much of Machiavelli's philosophy can be encapsulated by his famous words, "It is better to be feared than loved." Machiavelli believes that a person should attempt to gather and wield as much power as possible. Truth matters only as a person can use it to enhance one's reputation. Religion may be useful as it can provide a façade of respectability and trust.

Padgett, R. (1987). *The Handbook of Poetic Forms.* New York: Teachers & Writers Collaborative.

    A small book that describes and gives examples of several different kinds of poetry.

Films

Two homemade films were used as examples to demonstrate how to create titles without expensive editing equipment.

I showed the introduction of a homemade film made by a student who had typed out titles on stacks of white paper. He held the camera with one hand and with his other hand, he flipped through the pages. In another production, students arranged magnets on a refrigerator door. Each time the refrigerator door was opened, a new title appeared.

Nonfiction (Magazine Articles)

Ehrenreich, B. (1999, January). Nickel-and-Dimed. *Harper's,* 37–52.

Ehrenreich describes her life and times in Key West trying to make it as a sub-minimum-wage waitress. She describes a litany of interesting characters—the intelligent, illegal alien busboy; the tough, frazzled, and mercurial cook; the honest, hard-working, generous-spirited waitress-friend. Although she depicts the life among minimum-wage workers with sensitivity, empathy, and grace, the lifestyle comes off as an endless frenzy of day-to-day survival and heartache sometimes inexplicably punctuated by human kindness.

Grann, D. (2000, February 14). "Shooting Star: The Rise and Fall of a Basketball Legend." *The New Republic,* 22–29.

Grann describes the strange, but true, life story of a poor kid from the streets of Chicago—Leon Smith—who travels from orphanage to foster home to institution and back only to find himself one of the nation's hottest high school basketball prospects as a freshman. He is recruited to a private school in California, quits, re-enrolls at a public school in Chicago, and is eventually drafted by the Dallas Mavericks of the NBA out of high school. Along the way, his mother returns, his father tries to make contact, he finds love, loses it, and eventually winds up losing everything, except the support of a true friend.

Poems (most are available online)

Cohen, L. (1972). "Love Is a Fire." In *The Energy of Slaves.* Toronto: McClelland & Stewart.
Shakespeare, W. Sonnet 116 ("Let me not to the marriage of true minds . . . ")
Whitman, W. "When I Heard the Learn'd Astronomer."
Young, N. (1987). "Love Is a Rose." On *Linda Ronstadt's Greatest Hits.* Elektra Records.

Short Story

Lipsky, D. (1992). "Three Thousand Dollars." In Birmingham, J., Gilpin, L., and McCrindle, J., eds. *The Henfield Prize Stories.* New York: Warner Books, 151–164.

"Three Thousand Dollars" is about a young man going to college who receives $3,000 for college from his father. He blows the money, but doesn't tell his mother (who has been divorced from the father for quite some time). He plays the father against the mother to get the funds he needs for college and never owes up to his lying or responsibilities. He willingly (almost gladly) sacrifices his integrity and his relationships with his parents for the money.

OUTCOMES

1. A reticent, lazy football player decides to give a little effort.

2. An intelligent, aloof student finally explores her potential.

3. Students ponder love and the meaning of life.

4. Students read and discuss works by Shakespeare, Emerson, Jane Goodall, Albert Einstein, and several contemporary writers.

5. Students learn to write a pantoum.

6. Students write a philosophy of life, turn it into a film, then rewrite it.

7. Students use nonlinguistic inputs to enhance the quality of their writing.

ACTIVITIES

1. Go over clichés, lyrics, stories, and sayings about love.

2. Discuss the enduring nature of love

3. Recite Leonard Cohen's poem, "Love Is a Fire."

4. Recite Shakespeare's Sonnet 116.

5. Discuss the differences in the portrayals of love.

6. Recite Neil Young's "Love Is a Rose."

7. Have students read Emerson's essay, "The Conduct of Life."

8. Students select the most important passage from "The Conduct of Life" and discuss it.

9. Students define love and describe at least one aspiration.

10. Students read "Nickel-and-Dimed," a nonfiction piece about living on minimum wage.

11. Students discuss the relationship of money and ambition to love.

12. Students create a drawing based on their personal perspective on love, their philosophy of life, or the view of love espoused by a character from "Nickel-and-Dimed" or any of the writers whose works they have read.

13. Students write a pantoum to accompany the drawing.

14. Students read pantoums aloud while I walk around the room to show the related artwork.

15. Students read about the personal philosophies of Jane Goodall, Albert Einstein, Jeanne Kirkpatrick, Elie Wiesel, Niccolo Machiavelli, and Marcus Aurelius.

16. Students summarize the philosophies of an eminent individual and present their findings to class.

17. Students read "When I Heard the Learn'd Astronomer" by Walt Whitman.

18. Students read "Shooting Star," the story of the tribulations of a former number one draft pick in professional basketball.

19. Students discuss money and morality.

20. Students read a short story about money and morality entitled "Three Thousand Dollars."

21. Students write a paper describing their personal philosophies of life or love.

22. Students share their papers with class.

23. Students peer edit using the CIS (colors, images, and sounds) worksheet.

24. Students get together in groups, read each other's essays, and ponder a course of action.

25. Groups decide whether to adapt a single philosophy of life paper to film or to create a film depicting the philosophies of all group members.

26. I hand out an evaluation sheet and discuss how films will be graded.

27. I obtain camcorders from coaches and parents.

28. Students write screenplays, then film during class time and after school.

29. Groups edit their rough footage into a short film.

30. Groups show films to class.

31. Students vote on the most effective film.

32. Students translate the film back into an essay, using visual and auditory aspects of the film to bolster their writing.

33. Students present their papers to class.

CHAPTER

7

Naked and Fearless

"I wouldn't expect too much if I were you, this is a poor county." The ease with which many of my new colleagues spoke these words both disturbed me and comforted me. I wondered if perhaps I should lower my expectations. My colleagues were offering me acceptance if I achieved little—or nothing. The pressure was off; mediocrity seemed an acceptable standard. There was a certain comfort in this train of thought, and with this comfort came the doubt that if I tried to accomplish too much, I might come off looking foolish and burning myself out before I ever got started. On my first day of work I had reached a place in the road that a man named Frost had told me about. I took his advice, and thus far, that has made all the difference.

It was during my second year of teaching that I became cognizant of my own developing philosophy regarding education: That a teacher's successes and failures are predetermined by the expectations they have of their students. Seems like common sense, but I've learned that high expectations are not always a welcome philosophy.

I was hired by a principal who saw a need for change in a school that had been stagnating for years. At the time I was fresh out of college, and ready to accept the first job that was offered to me. The dropout rate at this school was one of the highest in the state, and assessment test scores were among the lowest. Teacher salaries were at the rock bottom of the pay scale, yet those who occupied positions with the school board and superintendent's office received some of the highest salaries in the state. The county was predominantly a welfare community where child abuse, spousal abuse, and domestic violence were everyday facts of life. And yet there were these students, these teenagers who were wonderfully creative, eager to learn, and responsive to new ideas.

In the teaching profession, life is much easier if you decide to make no waves. If you choose to keep your head down, teach to the script, and keep your students occupied with innocuous worksheets, chances are you will attain job security. You will also have had a career dull as spit. Although dull is certainly the easiest way to teach, it is not the highest and best use for a teacher. Effective teachers do not have to be entertaining or charismatic every second of the day. But they *should* have a good idea of individual capabilities and they should try their damnedest to get students to live up to their talents. The effort might involve coaxing, coddling, scolding, or getting out of the way. The moment and the students should dictate what happens next. What would you do in the following situation?

Scene from a Classroom

William's leg was bouncing rapidly under the table. His eyes were unfocused and a little wild. It was obvious from the smell that he hadn't bathed in some time. His usually dirty blonde hair was matted, his t-shirt yellow with dark stains. The ripped blue jeans were too short, revealing that he wore only one sock on his left foot. His right fist was clenching and unclenching. I called Marissa, a reliable, quiet freshman who sat up front, to my desk.

I spoke quietly. "Go tell Mrs. Huxley that William hasn't taken his medication."

Marissa knew, as did all the students, that William was "exceptional" and that he had medication he was supposed to be taking. She nodded her head and was gone.

Mrs. Huxley was the counselor. First period had not officially begun yet, and I wanted to get William out of my class before someone set him off. Mrs. Huxley would come and get William, and then call Grandma. From what I knew from Mrs. Huxley, William lived with Grandma, a kindly old lady who put three bullets into her daughter's head for lighting her (the daughter's) son on fire. Again. I liked Grandma and wanted to help William when I could. Today, I wouldn't be able to.

The bell rang and I surveyed the class. Austin, the seventeen-year-old freshman, was eyeing William. I stepped out in front of my podium from which I take roll and stared hard at Austin. It took only a moment for him to look at me. I mouthed the word *"don't"* and shook my head slowly. Austin's hand moved slowly to his pocket, and I knew he was putting whatever he was going to throw back in there.

Christa, who sat halfway back on the first row, suddenly began sobbing. Kelly, who sat on the opposite side of the room, quickly got up from her desk and moved toward Christa.

"SIT DOWN, KELLY!" My first words to the class.

Kelly stopped in her tracks and stared at me in shock. I couldn't help smiling. For three months now this had become a routine. Christa would fight with her boyfriend, sob in my class, and Kelly would take that as a sign to leave her seat and rush to Christa's side. The first time I had allowed it. The second time (the very next day) I had sent them both to the rest room (from which they did not return for the entire period). Now I was unsympathetic.

"Kelly, sit down. Christa, save it!"

Several of the other girls began snickering and Kelly exploded back to her seat, "I hate this class!"

Christa began sobbing louder just as Marissa came back in. Marissa took one look at her and rolled her eyes. She looked at me, nodded once, and took her seat. I glanced at William. He looked as if he were ready to blast off.

Just as I was ready to address the class and get things started, Melanie let out a blood-stopping scream. Several other girls screamed in response, but Melanie's was in earnest. She jumped from her seat and began slapping at her feet, legs, back, head, and shoulders.

I rushed down the row of desks screaming, "WHAT, WHAT!" and looked for anything that might possibly be killing Melanie. While she was dancing and slapping herself, one arm began jerking forward with an extended finger long enough for me to follow its line to the half-smashed remains of a twitching daddy longlegs that would not be long in this world. I grabbed a piece of binder paper from Logan's desk and wiped the twitching scene from the cracked tile floor beside Melanie's desk. I noticed that Melanie was wearing flip-flops. Flip-flops were against the dress code.

"That's why flip-flops are against the dress code, Melanie," I said as her slap dancing began to subside.

There was a gentle knock on my door and Mrs. Huxley came in, smiling. She went straight to William, looked closely into his eyes, then knelt down close beside him. She gathered his books, his bookbag, touched him gently on the shoulder, nodding and smiling all the time, and guided him out of the room. I had to marvel. If anybody else had touched William, he'd likely have bitten off their fingers.

So, what would you do? Hand out disciplinary referrals, do a little screaming, get students' minds back on conjunctions, assign extra work as punishment, throw your hands up in despair? Here's the end of the story.

Melanie, who was a pretty good student most of the time, had reclaimed her desk. She was staring at her desktop, her face flushed. I could tell that she was embarrassed. I smiled at her from the front of the class and nodded my head. "Spiders."

Her eyes closed, but her eyebrows lifted slightly and a visible shiver ran through her. She had given me an idea. I had planned an activity to work on subordinate clauses and conjunctions for the day, but I was always looking for openings when I thought students might be primed for something a little off the beaten path. Today we would awaken some monsters.

Deven, a pale, slight boy who was dyslexic, interrupted my thoughts. "What we doin' today, Mr. K.?"

"Monsters, Deven." The class quieted, and all eyes turned toward me.

"Monsters?" Christa was interested.

"Yeah, Christa, real mean ones." Now they were paying attention. I had only the vaguest notion of what I was doing at this point. Somewhere I had read about an activity where students created monsters and then drew pictures, and I was trying to recall how that had worked. Descriptive writing, yeah, it might work.

"I want you to get out a piece of paper and write a one-page description of the scariest monster you can imagine." I paused as the zippers, book bags, and binders began and ended their unique ruckus. "Mean monsters, okay? I want the writing to be crystal clear so that when someone else reads your description they can visualize your monster. I want lots of good adjectives."

"Does grammar count?" Leon, who was too young to be such a dedicated grade-grubber, would no doubt write me a boringly flawless essay on the Loch Ness, or Bigfoot, regardless of whether grammar counted or not.

"Yes, Leon, in your case I want to see several fragments done intentionally for effect."

Leon stared at me for a moment, then his eyes slanted up as he sorted through my words, looking for the appropriate file to reference them and allow comprehension. I stared at him patiently, knowing he would find it. He nodded one time to himself, his eyes coming back to me. "Very funny, Mr. K."

I watched the class as the morning's chaos visibly dissipated, and they became lost in their words. They were mine again for a short time. I wondered what type of monster William would have described were he present.

The Human Touch

When you teach naked, you look at students and curriculum through a humanistic lens. The vision of student potential is what keeps you hurtling forward.

When I first started out as a teacher, I used to try to cram all the information in curriculum guides, state-mandated tests, and answer-coded textbooks into the heads of my students. "This is boring, but we have to do it," was my mantra. The positive aspect of teaching to the test is that expectations are low and goals are attainable. Any student who possesses an IQ over 65 and practices test-taking skills can manage to pass a standardized high school graduation test. The 99 percent pass rates for driver's license exams in most states is proof enough that passing an exam does not by itself signify learning.

A student comes to class with certain talents and dispositions. Job one for a teacher is getting to know what a student can and cannot do and serving as leader of the class. An effective leader cannot be a wimp or a laggard. An effective leader must have a destination in mind, a plan of action, and enough courage to see it through.

Job two is getting students to turn on their brains and making learning interesting. Although some teachers readily abandon the idea of student engagement with the onset of the state assessment, most standardized tests purport to assess real learning. A student who loves writing and who writes with panache will do infinitely better on any standardized exam than one who loathes writing and attempts to mold his or her writing to fit a particular prefabricated design.

We have our medals and ribbons to show that the naked approach works. Year after year, some of the highest pass rates in the nation on the Advanced Placement exam for English come from Kunkel's classroom. When he was a secondary teacher, Baines's students won numerous writing awards, and their articles and stories appeared (and are still appearing) in journals, newspapers, and magazines around the country.

In this book, we have tried to provide you with a sense of what it feels like to teach naked. At the beginning of the year, you decide what you want students to be able to do by the end of the year. Then you create the experiences that will help students get there. Whether it is pondering childhood or alien cultures, producing screenplays or novels, exploring sixteen different kinds of writing, or creating the life of a fictional character, the secret to successful teaching is engaging students through the emotions and the intellect.

Assessment

So, how does someone who teaches naked grade students? It is difficult to generalize about assessment other than to say this: An assessment should identify specific weaknesses, praise strengths, and help foster an environment where students are unafraid to take wild risks. Assessment should help push students into what Vygotsky (1962) called *the zone of proximal development*. The zone is the playground where you want students to play.

When we evaluate student progress, we usually analyze products, presentations, and performances. Sometimes we create elaborate evaluation matrices with specific guidelines that we hand out prior to making an assignment. Sometimes we demand spontaneous shotgun responses that we evaluate holistically based upon execution (did the student pull off what he/she was trying to do?) and the quality of ideas (is the student trying to break some new ground with this effort?). Sometimes—and this is very important—we offer students our comments without a grade attached. Whenever we have them, we reach into our files to share samples of student work that we consider brilliant. Students like seeing the work of those who came before them, and it gives them an idea of what it takes to reach the A-level benchmark. We don't use a bell curve and we don't give out too many A's. We reserve the use of the A for when we think a student has maximized his or her performance on a particular assignment. Because it is rare that everyone in class achieves this on the same assignment, we usually end up giving a range of grades.

Learned Fearlessness

If you teach naked, you can expect to get some disapproving looks from the department chair, and you can expect to have some meetings with parents and administrators now and then. Whatever the occasion, we hope you will always welcome the chance to voice your platform—that your students possess vast potential and that you simply want to give them and the rest of the world a chance to glimpse the kinds of accomplishments of which they are capable.

When we taught the classes described in these chapters, it was an adventure for us as much as for our students. We taught with minds racing, eyes wide open, and hearts attuned to the moment at hand. Of course, we weren't always successful and our lessons were not always pretty, but no one ever questioned our sincerity or our results.

Naked teaching is more than an idea. An idea is something that you have, maybe in a fit of inspiration. Naked teaching is more like a vision. You don't have it; it has you. When you teach naked, you no longer have to spend the energy trying to become an effective teacher. The teacher becomes you.

R E F E R E N C E

Vygotsky, L.V. (1962). *Thought and Language.* Cambridge, MA: MIT Press.

8

The Hater Theory

Notes from a sixteen-year-old
on the prospect of real life
by Brian Harris

About Hater Theory and Brian, its author

At the time he wrote the following rant, Brian was an underachieving, gifted sixteen-year-old on the quiet side. He had no interest in grades, other than passing his classes, but probably had a little more ability than most. When Brian was challenged, he would come alive, ask penetrating questions, and produce creative work that went well beyond what was expected. Brian despised teachers who had no control, because their classes would quickly devolve into noisy goof-off sessions. In his mind, such teachers gave him no choice but to join in the chaos—they offered nothing better.

When Brian was interested in something, the world would vanish around him and he would become totally engrossed in the activity at hand. Outside of school, I knew Brian was an accomplished guitar player and pianist. I used to try to coax him into bringing his guitar to class and play, but he never did. One day late in the year, he dropped by after school when no one else was around and played for me. Truly, he had remarkable talent.

Brian worked evenings and weekends at a deli since his parents (great, involved parents) were not rich. Currently, Brian is majoring in film at a small liberal arts college in North Carolina.

The hater theory. That's life.

I'm sitting in my car reading when I see the first of about five hundred students walk through the front doors of the school. This is my cue. It's time to go inside. This is a routine I have mastered.

Roll down window if not already down, reach hand out door and grab handle. Open door slightly ajar so that no one notices. Retract hand and roll up window. Think to yourself, "I'm glad that these windows work." Turn off car. Open door.

Check the lock. If not locked, lock. Lean over seat and retrieve book bag from passenger side. Get out of car and pull book bag on your back. Adjust to comfort. Pull shirt down in the back so that the deep crevice of your ass is concealed. For extra protection pull up those boxers. Then pull up those pants. Check the door once more to see if it's locked. If not locked, lock. Close door and make your way across the parking lot.

Smile at the people that think you are their friend.

Smile at the people who can beat you up.

Smile at the people you will have to walk on.

Everyone's a politician.

Pass the alternative crowd, to which you bow your head in silent praise for anarchy. Tell yourself that you don't really care what they think about you. Keep walking. Suck in your gut as you as you pass the cheerleader parking section. Tell yourself that you don't really care what they think about you. Pass the coach and assistant principal under the awning in front of school. Smiling, ask, "How's it going?" Tell yourself that you don't really care what they think about you. Walk in the doors and hold them open for the person behind you. You have done your nice deed for the day. Switch to first person.

I walk in these halls and hear the teenage schoolhouse blues.

"Anton did not call me last night so I don't love him anymore."

"Susan gave Bill head at that party."

"I got caught smoking and my parents said I can't go out this weekend 'cause I'm grounded . . . what the hell is that about?"

"My puppy died."

Will you cry for me?

"My wallet is empty."

Will you cry for me?

"My friends all hate me."

Will you please cry for me?

And just as I am pulling out my harmonica to improvise a slow, sad solo, I am hit, full blast, like a target.

"Get yo bitch ass book bag out da middle of the goddamn hallway."

I try to think of how the comment can be taken intelligently. I give up.

"Excuse me." I say politely. This whole turn the other cheek concept is just too funny and I laugh to myself. The offended party mistakes the laughter as sarcasm and calls me a combination of four letter words, which only makes me laugh harder.

The first of sixteen bells rings, signifying I have six minutes to forget all aspects of life and turn into a walking data machine. At this task I often fail. The politicians are all walking around me, and I cannot help but hope someone else sees the charade.

I pass my friends. They take no notice. Most are heavily involved in the high school scene. I wave and get no response because I am a blur. Eyes are focused on the girl at the locker behind me or the guy walking two feet in front of me. I hide embarrassment with a "those darn kids" type of smile.

Tell yourself that you don't really care what they think about you.

I repeat the same process with three or four friends daily. Occasionally one sees me and smiles back or waves. These are good times. And I lie straight-faced.

This is the point. We are all these walking targets; seen through the barrel of society's Remington. We are all pretending to be something we aren't. I lie straight-faced because what I am, what I represent, is all false. It's just one aspect of the gigantic con surrounding us entitled "life" and occasionally, "the human spirit." Call it what you will, I am living in it and you are living in it. And morality, floating above us somewhere, is drinking a glass of champagne laced with cyanide giving a toast to the antagonist, hedonism, saying, "Job well done . . . Job well done."

This is high school in the nineties, only recently transformed into the zeros. I have to laugh at that. We're all zeros.

Homeroom is a joke.

Golden haired Tracy something or another is talking about the situation in Kosovo. She is quiet because the volume is turned down. I guess no one wants to know about some third world country split in half by warring cultures when we have our own hometown breakout of Tuberculosis.

"Does the shot hurt a lot?"

The shot, of course, is the vaccine to Tuberculosis. Tuberculosis being chronic or acute bacterial infection that primarily attacks the lungs, but which may also affect the kidneys, bones, lymph nodes, and brain. Yeah, no one wants to become an "infectee," as I heard one student refer to another; apparently the sick one had been walking among us, a horrible human abomination.

"Today, Serbs made an agreement to—" says golden haired Tracy from her little box in the corner.

"Nah, the shot felt nice."

In high school, sarcasm is God.

"The U.N. decided to—"

"Did you bleed when you got tested?"

"Bombs are being dropped in—"

"Yeah, I bled to death."

He's read his Bible, I think to myself.

"Hundreds of thousands died on Thurs—"

"I'm nervous."

"Watch channel one—but there is nothing to be nervous about anyway," the teacher interrupts.

Teachers know best.

I'm doing my history, taking on the Civil War, Kosovo, and the Tuberculosis all at once. Call me multitalented.

Another bell rings. History in the book bag. I can hear that blues chord progression coming out of classes everywhere, so I walk quickly. I paid five dollars for a locker I never use.

Two friends meet me in the hallway and ask about my weekend plans. I tell them I worked everyday and had no weekend. Otherwise, I lie straight-faced. I am hearing music in my head and don't feel the need to explain myself. I wonder why

I have so few friends. I wonder what it would be like to be the stereotypical teen-ager. But then I have never liked those *What Would Jesus Do* bracelets too much.

You say goodbye and take the corner. You enter the room and watch the wall or some other constant. If you watch something inanimate for long enough you can move it with your mind. At least I can. And I lie straight-faced as the bell rings. Forget the wall. Forget your life. Flip that switch that turns you into a data machine.

I earnestly try to listen in this class. I am plugged into the socket of knowl-edge . . . or something.

Second period is different.

I never quit watching the wall. And since it's a constant, I am moving it around the room. Beside me, beyond the broken wall lies a giant satellite, specifi-cally bought for the show we never watch. I wonder if in some other world, in a parallel dimension, Golden-haired Tracy something or another is still talking about wars and death. Right now, I can see through the window that the wind is blowing hard outside. The grass is swaying violently, but I seem to be the only one who notices.

"This is a horizontal asymptote," the Trigonometry Queen says not even noticing the two-ton wall just inches above her head.

"And this is a vertical asymptote."

And oops, lost concentration and the wall has fallen, crushing her into a small puddle of makeup and big shiny earrings. About this time I think about how appealing a trip to the bathroom might be.

The wall is back in place and the Trigonometry Queen preaches on about how we all need to know angles and vectors to succeed in life. She says that Trigonometry should be our ambition. I always think in present tense and at the moment, my ambition is about to break through the thin walls of my bladder.

"May I go to the bathroom?"

Sour looks from the Queen. Please forgive me if I have offended thee.

The bathrooms are clean, and I lie straight-faced. Paint drips in heavy clumps over the scribblings of the "Shit Poet." I think that is what he is called in this stall. This is recreation in high school. Whenever boredom strikes, it's nice to walk from stall to stall and admire the diversity of our student population. While performing the simple act of urinating, I can learn where to get a blowjob, where to go to get my ass kicked, who to ask for confirmation, and even what guys prefer penises to vaginas. Two stalls over someone has scratched "John 3:16" and "Jesus saves" right next to the school whore's phone number.

Sometimes you have to wonder about the line between evangelism and an oxymoron.

Back in class, you find time for anything besides work. I'm busy levitating a wall over the class clown. I laugh at his jokes because everyone else does.

Tell yourself that you don't really care what they think about you.

I used to be the class-clown until I matured, or maybe that was everyone else. In high school, you learn how to become what you are expected to be.

The bell rings and the wall falls right back into place. Too bad.

Jump to third period. Here we are all engrossed. This is history and my teacher that cusses. The reconstruction is our topic, and I have to wonder, did Robert E. Lee ever think he would be taught in lectures interrupted by announcements for T.B. tests?

"Sherman's march burned thousands—"

You hear a beep. A crack. A voice.

"Would all students in homeroom 11c and 11d—Mrs. So 'n So's or Mr. So 'n So's homeroom—please report to the auxiliary gym. Mr. So 'n So's class go to the right door and Mrs. So 'n So go to the left door.

A crack.

Students are up and moaning.

You realize Sherman never quit marching.

"Many Georgia citizens still hate Sherman to this day because of his—"

"Does the test hurt a lot?"

"No it feels nice."

In high school, repetition is Matthew, Mark, Luke and John.

"Sherman, guys."

You have to laugh at failed attempts.

"Is the needle big?"

"Houses were burned."

Sherman's old news. The needle is our new fascination.

The faceless voice interrupts Sherman over and over and over and over and over.

You wonder if you had family in Georgia at the time of Sherman. You wonder, if so, did they too have to take a T.B. test.

Somewhere, in this deep state of contemplation, you wonder, "How did I ever get to this point? Where did I go wrong?"

My ambition is to be a child again, sitting on the front steps of my house, selling rocks broken to shine a belly of quartz. I swore they were the lost diamonds of Rome. I swore I would never make a B in high school. I swore I would be a lawyer. I swore I would never turn my back on a friend.

Now I am seventeen and failing Chemistry. Now I am seventeen and have no future. Now I am seventeen, stomping on my friends' bleeding hearts to make myself feel a little better.

You swear a lot of things as a child.

You hear your name. Apparently, Sherman's still marching. Yes, of course, you were paying attention.

And just as Sherman is raping another poor Georgia woman, one of the 16 bells rings. Get up and go. Walk to teacher and swear once more you were paying attention. Maybe you were. Walk to next class.

The blues are louder now. Three periods have added verses and a loud, melodious chorus. Under the roar of the singers, I hear that old one, four, five, chord progression. My hand is at my side holding a snap that usually dangles from my book bag. I click the snap to the beat inside my head. Around me in the hallways, students gather in a frantic communion. Every conversation has a different subject, but it's all the same music.

Will you please cry for me?

I get to class early, the same room as first period. The wall is back in place. Now, rather than white bricks, I decide to stare at the posters hanging around the room. These are nice posters.

APPENDIX

If you have a principal who hears about you teaching naked during class, you might need some help if you get called on the carpet. The national standards formulated by NCTE (National Council of Teachers of English) and IRA (International Reading Association) provided a foundation for state departments of education as they developed their own, state-centric versions of the standards.

The activities listed at the end of each chapter in this book have been correlated to each of the national standards that follows. Although reading the list won't give you goose bumps of inspiration, most administrators should be suitably impressed. It is within the realm of possibility that some administrators might realize the kind of results you are after and get off your back long enough to let you achieve them. Of course, once the soaring scores of your students roll in, you will likely be asked to provide in-service instruction for every teacher in the district on "the fundamentals of teaching naked." So, be ready.

1. Students read a wide range of print and nonprint texts to build an understanding of texts, of themselves, and of the cultures of the United States and the world; to acquire new information; to respond to the needs and demands of society and the workplace; and for personal fulfillment. Among these texts are fiction and nonfiction, classic and contemporary works.

   > Chapter 1, activities 2, 7, 12.
   > Chapter 2, activities 1, 8, 10, 14.
   > Chapter 3, activities 6, 7, 8, 9, 15, 17, 20.
   > Chapter 4, activities 1, 2, 4, 15.
   > Chapter 5, activities 9, 15.
   > Chapter 6, activities 1, 3, 4, 6, 7, 10, 15, 17, 18, 20, 32, 33.

2. Students read a wide range of literature from many periods in many genres to build an understanding of the many dimensions (e.g., philosophical, ethical, aesthetic) of human experience.

   > Chapter 1, activities 2, 4, 7, 12.
   > Chapter 2, activities 1, 8, 10, 14.
   > Chapter 3, activities 6, 7, 8, 9, 15, 17, 20.
   > Chapter 4, activities 1, 8, 15.
   > Chapter 5, activities 9, 15.
   > Chapter 6, activities 1, 3, 4, 6, 7, 10, 15, 17, 18, 20, 32, 33.

3. Students apply a wide range of strategies to comprehend, interpret, evaluate, and appreciate texts. They draw on their prior experience, their interactions with other readers and writers, their knowledge of word meaning and of

other texts, their word identification strategies, and their understanding of textual features (e.g., sound–letter correspondence, sentence structure, context, graphics).

> Chapter 1, activities 4, 7, 10, 12.
> Chapter 2, activities 1, 5, 7, 8, 10, 14.
> Chapter 3, activities 2, 6, 7, 8, 9, 21.
> Chapter 4, activities 1, 2, 7, 8, 15, 18, 29.
> Chapter 5, activities 4, 9, 15.
> Chapter 6, activities 1, 3, 4, 6, 7, 8, 10, 15, 17, 18, 20, 23, 32, 33.

4. Students adjust their use of spoken, written, and visual language (e.g., conventions, style, vocabulary) to communicate effectively with a variety of audiences and for different purposes.

> Chapter 1, activities 3, 4, 7, 8, 9, 10, 12, 13.
> Chapter 2, activities 5, 6, 7, 9, 12.
> Chapter 3, activities 4, 5, 6, 13, 14, 19, 22.
> Chapter 4, activities 6, 10, 15, 17, 19, 20, 21, 22, 25, 26, 30.
> Chapter 5, activities 11, 12, 13.
> Chapter 6, activities 13, 16, 21, 23, 28, 32, 33.

5. Students employ a wide range of strategies as they write, using different writing process elements appropriately to communicate with different audiences for a variety of purposes.

> Chapter 1, activities 3, 8, 10, 11, 13.
> Chapter 2, activities 3, 4, 5, 6, 9, 12.
> Chapter 3, activities 4, 5, 6, 13, 14, 19, 22.
> Chapter 4, activities 6, 10, 12, 15, 19, 20, 21, 22, 25, 26, 30.
> Chapter 5, activities 11, 12.
> Chapter 6, activities 9, 14, 16, 21, 28, 32, 33.

6. Students apply knowledge of language structure, language conventions (e.g., spelling and punctuation), media techniques, figurative language, and genre to create, critique, and discuss print and nonprint texts.

> Chapter 1, activities 3, 7, 8, 10, 11, 12, 13.
> Chapter 2, activities 5, 9, 12.
> Chapter 3, activities 2, 4, 5, 6, 13, 14, 19, 22.
> Chapter 4, activities 6, 10, 15, 19, 20, 21, 22, 26, 30.
> Chapter 5, activities 4, 5, 11, 12.
> Chapter 6, activities 14, 16, 21, 28, 32, 33.

7. Students conduct research on issues and interests by generating ideas and questions, and by posing problems. They gather, evaluate, and synthesize data

from a variety of sources (e.g., print and nonprint texts, artifacts, people) to communicate their discoveries in ways that suit their purpose and audience.

> Chapter 1, activities 7, 10, 11, 13.
> Chapter 2, activities 9, 11, 12.
> Chapter 3, activities 6, 12, 13, 14, 19, 22.
> Chapter 4, activities 6, 9, 15, 21, 22, 26, 30.
> Chapter 5, activities 11, 12, 13.
> Chapter 6, activities 14, 16, 21, 28, 32, 33.

8. Students use a variety of technological and information resources (e.g., libraries, databases, computer networks, video) to gather and synthesize information and to create and communicate knowledge.

> Chapter 2, activities 6, 9, 11, 12.
> Chapter 3, activities 3, 6, 12, 13, 14, 19, 22.
> Chapter 4, activities 6, 9, 13, 14, 15, 17, 23, 26, 27, 28.
> Chapter 5, activities 5, 14.
> Chapter 6, activities 12, 21, 28, 32.

9. Students develop an understanding of and respect for diversity in language use, patterns, and dialects across cultures, ethnic groups, geographic regions, and social roles.

> Chapter 1, activities 2, 3, 4, 7, 8, 12, 13.
> Chapter 2, activities 7, 9, 12.
> Chapter 3, activities 5, 6, 12, 13, 14, 19, 22.
> Chapter 4, activities 6, 9, 15, 19, 20, 22, 28.
> Chapter 5, activities 11, 12.
> Chapter 6, activities 14, 16, 21, 28, 32, 33.

10. Students whose first language is not English make use of their first language to develop competency in the English language arts and to develop understanding of content across the curriculum.

None of the activities in *Naked Teaching* are explicitly designed for use by students whose first language is not English. However, most activities could be readily adapted for ESOL.

11. Students participate as knowledgeable, reflective, creative, and critical members of a variety of literacy communities.

If you teach naked, you utilize groups effectively and you create an environment in which students want to participate. Often, students seem to learn as much from each other as they do from the teacher. All activities in this book strive to build a community of enthusiastic, insightful learners.

12. Students use spoken, written, and visual language to accomplish their own purposes (e.g., for learning, enjoyment, persuasion, and the exchange of information).

   When students see the value in an activity and exert their best efforts, they are learning because they want to. Then, teaching is a blast.

13. Okay, okay. I know what you are thinking. So what if there are only twelve official national standards? The thirteenth standard is a Baines/Kunkel special: Students listen carefully (to the teacher and each other) and think deeply about what it means to be human on planet Earth in the twenty-first century. Let's hope your principal doesn't need any justification for this one.